SURVIVING

COPING WITH A LIFE CRISIS

SURVIVING

COPING WITH A LIFE CRISIS

Dr. BOB MONTGOMERY
and Dr. LAUREL MORRIS

FISHER
BOOKS™

Publishers	Helen V. Fisher
	Howard W. Fisher
Managing Editor	Sarah Trotta
Editor	Melanie Mallon
Book Design & Production	Randy Schultz
Cover Design	David Constable

Published by Fisher Books, LLC
5225 W. Massingale Road
Tucson, Arizona 85743-8416
(520) 744-6110
www.fisherbooks.com

Printed in U.S.A.
5 4 3 2 1

**Library of Congress
Cataloging-in-Publication Data**

Montgomery, Bob, 1943-
  Surviving : coping with a life crisis /
  Bob Montgomery and Laurel
  Morris.— North American ed.
    p. cm.
Originally published: Melbourne :
  Lothian, 1989.
Includes bibliographical references
  and index.
  ISBN 1-55561-239-3
  1. Life change events—Psychological
  aspects. 2. Loss (Psychology) 3.
  Adjustment (Psychology) 4. Stress
  management. I. Morris, Laurel.
  II. Title.
BF637.L53 M66 2000
155.9'3—dc21   99-054870

First published in Australia, 1989, by Thomas C. Lothian Pty. Ltd.
Copyright © Dr. Bob Montgomery & Dr. Laurel Morris 1989

Note: The information in this book is true and complete to the best of our
knowledge. The information in this book is general and is offered with no
guarantees on the part of the authors or Fisher Books. The authors and
publisher disclaim all liability in connection with the use of this book.
The names and identifying details of people associated with events
described in this book have been changed. Any similarity to actual
persons is coincidental.

The authors gratefully acknowledge Albert Ellis and Dr. Robert Harper for
permission to reproduce "10 popular irrational beliefs" from *New Guide to
Rational Living,* and Dr. Aaron Beck for permission to reproduce the list
of "Common Mistakes in Thinking."

Contents

Introduction vii

1 The Human Reactions to Crisis 1
The Crisis Response and Recovery Cycle • *The crisis response*
• *Release or escape* • *Recovery* • *Friends and family*

2 Coping with Personal Disasters 13
Violent Crime • *Initial impact* • *Recoil* • *Resolution*
• *Severity of reaction—five factors* • *Nonvictims and violent crime*
• Rape • *Nonvictims and rape* • *Rape and the law*
• Prolonged Terror • Torture • Accidents

3 Coping with Death and Grief 33
Your Own Death • *Living with dying* • *Coping to the end*
• *Managing chronic pain* • Grief • *The grief response*
• *When grief goes wrong* • *Suggestions for managing grief*
• *Coping with the death of a child* • *Grieving for the unborn*
• *Coping with loss from suicide*

4 Coping with Marital and Family Crises 57
Family Conflict, Arguments and Fights • *Family fights*
• *Battered spouses* • *Battered children* • *Sexual abuse and
incest* • *Adolescent disasters* • *Discovering an affair*

5 Coping with Life-Stage Crises 79
Midlife Crisis • *Setting life goals* • Depression during
Menopause • Moving • Losing Your Job

6 Coping with Large-Scale Disasters 99
The Stages of a Disaster • *Before the disaster* • *During
the disaster* • *After the disaster* • Natural versus Man-Made
Disasters • Post-Traumatic Stress Disorders • Your Recovery
• Preparing for Crises • Rescuers Can Be Victims
• *Critical-incident stress debriefing*

7 Coping with Any Crisis 117
Accept Your Normal Reactions • Share Your Feelings
• *Group sharing* • Get Organized • Use Your Resources
• *Helpful organizations* • Drugs? • Depression, Guilt,
Anger, Mood Swings, Sleep Problems • What Did It All Mean?

8 How to Manage Your Emotional Reactions 133
Feeling Better by Thinking Straighter • *The coping statement*
• Mental Relaxation: Step by Step • *Say the coping statement
to yourself* • *And back it up with constructive action* • *Teach
yourself to think rationally* • *What was your original self-talk?*
• *Test your self-talk for mistakes* • *Look for the underlying
irrational beliefs* • *Now practice a more rational view*
• Do You Need a Calming Response?

9 How to Share Your Feelings Constructively 161
Leveling • *The X-Y-Z formula* • *When not to level* • Asking
for Changes in Behavior • Listening • Validating • Body Talk
• But This Is So Artificial!

**10 Coping with the Big Three:
Depression, Anger, Guilt** 179
Depression • *Physical treatments for depression*
• *The causes of depression* • *Managing your depression*
• *Suicide?* • Anger • *What is anger?* • *When is anger
a problem?* • *External causes of anger* • *Internal causes
of anger* • *Behavioral causes of anger* • *Managing your
anger* • *Stopping arguments* • Guilt

11 Sleeping Better 199
What Is Sleep? • How Much Sleep Do You Need? • What
Disturbs Your Sleep? • *Biological factors* • *Psychological
factors* • *Drug use* • *Bad sleep habits or environments*
• *Conditioning* • Managing Your Sleep Better

Resources 215

Introduction

This book is for people who are trying to cope with a life crisis. The crisis may be prolonged, such as a life-threatening illness or an impending death, or, as in most cases, the crisis may have occurred suddenly or unexpectedly—after it's over, those involved are stuck trying to handle the aftereffects. Such crises include being a victim or even a witness of an assault, rape, burglary or accident; having someone close to you die unexpectedly, possibly by suicide; being involved in a natural disaster such as a tornado, flood or earthquake; being involved in a large-scale accident, such as a train or airplane crash; experiencing or losing a loved one to a shooting incident, such as those occurring in United States schools; losing a relationship through separation and divorce; or getting fired, transferred or laid off.

This is not an exhaustive list of possible life crises. A *life crisis* is any event that causes you to experience unusually strong emotional reactions that interfere with your ability to function, at the time or in the future. Even winning a lottery can be psychologically disruptive; this seemingly desirable event triggers a lot of problems for some people. We outline detailed approaches for coping with the more common life crises, but first we explain the general pattern of how people respond to a crisis and what a person can do to cope better. So even if you are facing an unusual crisis, you can adapt our general approach to your specific situation.

> *We emphasize now, and will repeat, that the physical and emotional reactions that develop in response to a crisis are normal.*

This book is primarily a self-help manual for people who are themselves coping with a personal crisis. *We emphasize now, and will repeat, that the physical and emotional reactions that develop in response to a crisis are normal.* These reactions are primitive responses of the body and mind that humans have evolved to help them survive a crisis. Accepting that their stress reactions to a crisis are normal is an essential step to enable victims to cope effectively with that crisis. Helping victims understand their experiences and accept their reactions is the first goal of this book.

Although stress reactions to a crisis are normal, they have the potential to cause problems if they continue for too long. High levels of stress cause fatigue, interfere with your performance of everyday tasks and make you more susceptible to illness. Stress reactions to a crisis can lead to life-long problems if they aren't handled effectively. Life-long problems are a particular risk for the crisis victim who denies her reactions or misinterprets them as unusual. So the second goal of this book is to provide self-help instructions on how to manage those stress reactions effectively, once you have accepted their normality.

This book will also help people who are trying to help the victim of a crisis. You may be a friend or relative who can see the victim's suffering but just don't know what you can do to help. The suggestions in this book will help you support victims, without unintentionally adding to their problems. As you will learn, sometimes the best-intended but misguided actions have the worst effects. And, of course, you can suggest to the victim that she work through the book herself.

As you will learn, sometimes the best-intended but misguided actions have the worst effects.

This book should also be helpful to counselors, psychologists, psychiatrists, social workers and other mental-health professionals in the position to help crisis victims. It will provide both a model of the common stress reactions to crisis and a practical program for helping victims manage those reactions. This book should complement face-to-face counseling by providing supportive information and clear practical advice that will reduce the client's dependence on the professional counselor and enhance the cost-effectiveness of professional help.

Clinical experience suggests that crisis victims benefit most if supportive counseling is provided soon after the crisis, ideally within twenty-four to forty-eight hours, especially after sudden or unexpected crises. The longer that support is delayed, the less effective it will be, and the more likely it is that the victim will develop long-term problems requiring a different, long-term therapeutic approach.

Professor Jeffrey Mitchell, of the Emergency Health Services Program at the University of Maryland, relates the example of a disaster in which a North Sea drilling platform broke up in a storm with considerable loss of life. The survivors were brought to shore in two groups, which arrived several hours apart. The first group received immediate counseling and today are well-adjusted and functioning normally. Most have returned to their former jobs. The second group heard that the first group received counseling and decided that seeing a counselor was a sign of weakness. They refused similar counseling on their arrival. Many members of this group are still suffering from a variety of physical and psychological problems and have been unable to return to their old jobs, even though some of them received counseling several months after the event.

This situation illustrates that the sooner a crisis victim receives effective supportive counseling, face-to-face or through a self-help program like this book, the less time her normal stress reactions will last and the less emotional or mental deterioration she'll experience. If you are a victim yourself, or you are trying to help one, the sooner you start a structured program of support, the better. Groups of people at significant risk of becoming victims, such as emergency service personnel or the armed forces, should undergo a preventive educational program as a routine part of training. They should also make arrangements for a quick-response supportive-counseling facility to operate immediately after a crisis. We should insist that our communities provide quick-response supportive counseling that can respond immediately to large-scale crises. The cost of providing such facilities would be offset by the savings of avoiding long-term problems for victims who receive inadequate, belated or no counseling. We offer suggestions for preventive training and quick-response supportive counseling in chapter 6.

Professor Mitchell believes that supportive counseling is only minimally effective by six weeks after a crisis. This does not mean that there is nothing useful you can do if more than six weeks have elapsed since your crisis. It does mean that what you need to do may be different, and may require more effort, for you to overcome the extra effects resulting from taking no immediate action. If you are trying self-help, concentrate on chapters 8, 9 and 10 (which are more therapeutic than other chapters). Chapters 1 and 7 will be less helpful to you because they focus on providing supportive counseling. Solid and persistent effort to try the suggestions in chapters 8, 9 and 10 may help you successfully help yourself.

You may decide self-help is not going to work for you, perhaps after you've tried it, or perhaps because it looks like too much work even to start. Then you owe it to yourself to get professional help, such as consulting a qualified clinical psychologist. (In the United States, look for a clinical psychologist who is board certified by the American Board of Clinical Health Psychology, an affiliated board of the American Board of Professional Psychology. In Canada, look for a psychologist who is accredited by the Canadian Psychological Association or who has a postgraduate qualification in clinical psychology.)

The key to coping healthfully with a crisis is to work through your reactions so that they gradually diminish and eventually you can come to terms with your crisis experience.

We have already emphasized that the stress reactions occurring because of a crisis are normal. In chapter 1 we describe how people normally experience and progress through those reactions, and in chapter 7 we offer you suggestions on how to work through those reactions. *The key to coping healthfully with a crisis is to work through your reactions so that they gradually diminish and eventually you can come to terms with your crisis experience*. Then you can get on with your life, changed in ways, but not significantly hindered. Victims develop serious problems when they do not go through this normal progression, either because they have tried to deny their reactions from the start or because they found working on them so painful that they got stuck. Then it's time for professional help.

Friends and family can provide crucial emotional support for your attempts to work through your stress reactions. But if your attempts to do it yourself have not been enough, it is unlikely that any of your friends or family will have the necessary training and skills to help you get unstuck. However well-intended, a clumsy attempt to help you get in touch with how you really felt during and after the crisis may provoke an intense emotional reaction that is distressing if not dangerous to you. On top of this, your reaction may simply overwhelm your untrained helper. We encourage you to seek out and accept the emotional support available from friends, family and associates, but if you decide you need practical advice as well, talk to a qualified counselor.

1

The Human Reactions to Crisis

We define a *crisis* as any situation that causes you to experience unusually strong emotional reactions that interfere with your ability to function, at the time or in the future. To cause unusually strong emotions, the typical crisis is itself an unusual event, at least in any one person's life, although some people may have occupations or lifestyles that put them more at risk of a crisis than most of us. If you have observed people during or after a crisis, you may have noticed the many differences in their reactions. One person stays cool as a cucumber, dealing methodically with the situation, while another becomes hysterical, floundering helplessly. One person appears calm and even detached at the time but is angry or depressed a week later.

One person stays cool as a cucumber, dealing methodically with the situation, while another becomes hysterical, floundering helplessly.

This variability in human reactions is true for all of psychology, of course, not just for reactions to crisis. Each of us is a unique individual with a unique way of responding to the world. This diversity in humans is what makes us so interesting. Yet through this diversity you can see patterns and trends—a picture with some order to it. This is essential if psychology is to make sense of its subject matter. If each individual were not just unique, but totally unlike all other humans, then we would have nothing to compare her to and it would take forever to understand and help just that one troubled person.

As psychologists, we look for underlying patterns so we can make sense of the variety of human behavior, thoughts and feelings and therefore develop effective, practical ways to help different people. When we look for these patterns, we miss out on some of the rich individuality of each person, but we come up with ideas and procedures that are likely to apply to many persons. In other words, psychologists can come up with notions about human behavior, thoughts and feelings that will be more or less right for most people but probably not dead right for any one person. The fit between our ideas and one person is usually close enough for us to offer practical help, without ever pretending or even aiming to understand this one person fully.

Our reasons for approaching the individual by using the patterns of people in general are important for you to keep in mind while reading this chapter. When we describe the ways people typically react during and after a crisis, we are not describing how they *always* or *should* react. Pop psychologists in recent years have addressed the psychology of death, dying and grief by suggesting that there is a single, normal and desirable pattern for coping with these crises. While we applaud anyone willing to take on the topic of death and grief, which have been taboo topics for so long, we are sure this simplistic approach has caused unnecessary worry in people whose reactions were different—*normally* different.

One of the most typical characteristics of human psychology is its *variability*, our tendency to be a little different from each other and from any general description of how people are or should be. One of the main goals of this chapter is to help you understand and accept the normality of your stress reactions to your crisis. We don't want to sabotage that goal by making you worry if your reactions don't exactly match our description. If you are still concerned that your reactions are abnormal in some way, after you have read this chapter and kept in mind our emphasis on the *normal* variability of human reactions, then it might be time to seek a professional opinion. A qualified mental-health professional should help you pinpoint any unusual problem we don't cover in this book and help you to do something about it or reassure you that your reactions are normal. But don't tell yourself that your reactions are so strange or unacceptable that you can't admit them to someone else. That would be exactly the kind of denial and bottling up that may lead to serious problems later.

The Crisis Response and Recovery Cycle

When a person is a victim of a life crisis, he goes through a process we call the *Crisis Response and Recovery Cycle (CRRC)*. This is simply a description of how people *usually* respond to and recover from a crisis. The Crisis Response and Recovery Cycle has three main stages: crisis response, release or escape, and recovery cycle. These are summarized in the table below.

The crisis response
A *crisis response* is the immediate response to the unfolding crisis. This response lasts as long as the crisis and may include shock, disbelief, realization and a non-emotional survival state.

The Crisis Response and Recovery Cycle (CRRC)

1. Crisis response	3. Recovery cycle
• Shock	• Shock
• Disbelief	• Depression
• Realization	• Mood swings
• Non-emotional survival state	• Anger
	• Philosophical reflection
2. Release or escape	• Laying to rest

Shock

In most cases, a victim will have been going about her normal daily life when the crisis occurred or began. The unexpected nature of the crisis initially produces a shock reaction. Shock can affect those experiencing an ongoing crisis, such as coping with a life-threatening illness or impending death or being held hostage for a long time, because there is usually one moment when the person is first aware of the crisis. At this moment, a person may experience shock. Shock can also affect people who are regularly in hazardous situations, such as emergency personnel. A hazardous situation may seem routine until it develops to the point where a person realizes that it is actually or potentially out of control and has become a crisis. The unexpected and unusual nature of the event, or of developments within the situation, can trigger shock.

One of the physiological components of shock is the withdrawal of blood supply from the outer parts of the body. This causes the white face of someone in shock. The brain also loses blood supply, which can cause nausea and dizziness, perhaps fainting. Breathing may become fast and shallow, possibly irregular, while one's heart rate usually speeds up.

If the crisis is extremely frightening, a person may lose control over the muscles of the bladder and bowel. Although many people joke about someone wetting or soiling his pants in a crisis, you should understand that these are involuntary responses produced by the overwhelming stimulation of the situation and are not due to any lack of nerve or courage.

In our opinion, the truly brave person is the one who keeps going despite being terrified.

In our opinion, the truly brave person is the one who keeps going despite being terrified. Feeling no fear in a threatening situation doesn't show bravery—some stupidity, maybe, but not bravery.

Disbelief

Because crises are unusual and unexpected events, it is not surprising that your first reaction may be disbelief: "This just can't be happening, at least not to me." This initial disbelief may be a coping mechanism used by the mind to protect itself from the full impact of the crisis. Just as the shock reaction is a primitive attempt by the body to protect itself from damage, this initial denial of the reality of the crisis may give the mind breathing space to come to grips with the enormity of what is happening.

Realization

But the crisis continues, and disbelief gives way to the realization that this event is really happening, is not imaginary or "some kind of joke." This realization may be accompanied by an intensification of the shock response. In any but a brief crisis, realization will usually trigger the fourth component of the crisis response: the non-emotional survival state.

The non-emotional survival state

During this stage a victim's emotions become frozen or flat. Many people later remark on how calm they were at the time of most danger. In this apparently non-emotional state, your thinking is focused entirely on one issue: survival. In this state, a victim will do almost anything he thinks will help him survive. Sometimes this produces actions that he later regrets.

We have all seen movies like the James Bond series in which the hero escapes from impossibly threatening situations, through a combination of quick thinking, dexterity, strength and boldness. Most of us have imagined ourselves being equally resourceful and brave if we were ever to be in a tough spot. The truth, as those who have really been in a crisis can testify, is very different. The numbing effects of the shock and the emotionally frozen focus on survival at all costs don't exactly pave the way for heroic action. If the crisis is a lengthy robbery, assault or hostage situation, most victims will cooperate with the perpetrators. In chapter 2 we explain in more detail how this cooperation can even result in a victim identifying with the aggressor, a phenomenon called the *Stockholm syndrome.* Even if a victim's reaction is not so extreme, she may still assist the aggressor in some way, understandably believing this increases her chances of survival. Later she may feel guilty about these actions, particularly if others criticize her for them.

Most crisis victims will stay in this non-emotional survival state until the crisis is over, depending on its duration. During a long-term crisis, such as the terminal illness of a close relative, the victim is usually able to escape psychologically from the crisis from time to time by being involved in other activities, slipping back into the non-emotional survival state when again having to confront the ongoing crisis.

Release or escape

Eventually the victim escapes from the crisis. An attacker leaves; a captor releases you; the fire is put out; the seriously ill person dies; rescue workers free you. In terms of our definition of a crisis, the event that has caused your unusually strong emotions ends, at least for you. While this release from the immediate crisis is naturally welcome, it leaves you with a task that most people are unprepared for and even unaware of—the need to cope with the emotional aftereffects of having been in a crisis.

Recovery cycle

Recovering from the emotional disturbance of having been a crisis victim is the third stage of the Crisis Response and Recovery Cycle. Even with immediate supportive counseling and good emotional support from family and friends, full recovery may take weeks or months, depending on the severity of the crisis and the individual's psychological resources. Without immediate supportive counseling, or emotional support, or at least appropriate therapy later, the victim may never completely recover and may have life-long problems as a consequence of the crisis. The usual components of the recovery phase are shock, depression, mood swings, anger, philosophical reflection and laying to rest.

Shock

Immediately after a crisis is over, most victims will go into a state of shock again. This state can last from a few hours to several days, depending on the severity of the crisis. This period of shock is often marked by a dull, flat emotional state. While shock probably protects the victim from the immediate impact of the crisis, others often misinterpret it as meaning the victim is not distressed but is okay. Friends and family may actively but unwisely encourage this illusion with reassurances, such as "Forget it, now that it's over." They will then be unprepared and alarmed when the victim's feelings start to emerge later.

Depression

After the shock phase of recovery, many victims become depressed, an understandable reaction to their experiences. At this point, the victim may be unable express anger about his experiences, which can lead to depression. During this depression, a victim may withdraw within himself, breaking off close relationships and isolating himself from family or friends. They in turn can unintentionally make the depression worse by encouraging the victim to deny it or by encouraging the victim to dwell on it unnecessarily. Some people will avoid contact with a victim, perhaps in an attempt to reassure themselves that such a crisis could not happen to them. This, of course, only adds to the victim's emotional isolation.

> *Some people will avoid contact with a victim, perhaps in an attempt to reassure themselves that such a crisis could not happen to them.*

Mood swings

Toward the end of the depression phase, many victims experience marked mood swings, up one day and down the next. These mood swings can cause extreme anxiety if the victim, or those around her, misinterpret them as being an abnormal or undesirable reaction. It is important to understand that these mood swings are a *normal* reaction during the recovery stage of the Crisis Response and Recovery Cycle. They will pass more quickly if everyone accepts them as normal and no one tries to resist them.

Anger

Following the depression phase, perhaps while still experiencing mood swings, most victims become actively angry. Although this anger may be difficult for both victims and those around them, it does mark progress through the recovery stage. In a sense, the victim is angry at what has happened to him, however irrational it might seem to be angry about an unforeseeable or accidental event. In doing so, he is moving out of the role of helpless victim toward trying to grapple actively with the world again.

If there is no "logical" target for this anger—the attacker has not been caught or no one was really responsible for the accident—it may be displaced onto a friend, family member or associate. The victim may see the recipient as a "safe" object to attack or he may target this particular person simply because he's there. During a long-term crisis, family, friends or authorities may bear the brunt of this anger for not rescuing the victim sooner. Someone on the receiving end of a victim's anger can easily become distressed herself, particularly because the anger will seem unfair. Angry or defensive responses to the victim's anger may provoke further anger, or encourage the victim again to try to deny his feelings because of the effect they are having on others.

Someone on the receiving end of a victim's anger can easily become distressed herself, particularly because the anger will seem unfair.

Philosophical reflection

Many victims will begin to reflect on their crisis, trying to make sense of it and what it means to them. Being a victim of a crisis can bring home three basic truths, facts that humans generally find so uncomfortable that they usually ignore or deny them.

First is the fact that each of us is always vulnerable. At any moment, any one of us might be struck down by some force, no matter how strong or brave or healthy or smart or good we might have been. There are forces in life we cannot protect ourselves from, at least not completely. Second is the related fact that death is inevitable, sooner or later. And third is the fact that life events can occur at random. There really is a factor called "luck," over which we have little or no control.

The combination of these truths is distinctly uncomfortable—so uncomfortable that most of the time we live as if they were not true. This self-delusion is necessary for us to function normally. If during every waking moment your mind was occupied with the possibility that in the next second your life could be turned upside down or you could be injured or killed, then you would be in such a constant state of anxiety, you wouldn't function properly. So, most of the time, we act as if this possibility of random crisis does not exist.

Humans seem to be the only species who are consciously aware of the nature and inevitability of death. Some other species show signs of apparent distress when they are confronted with a life-threatening situation or the death of

> *Humans seem to be the only species who are consciously aware of the nature and inevitability of death.*

one of their kind but, as far as we know, they don't think as humans do, and so cannot think about death in its absence. We can, and that usually makes us uncomfortable. Some people are able to reduce their fear of death through their religious beliefs, but most of us are disturbed by it, especially the prospect of our own. So we acknowledge it intellectually but act as if it isn't going to happen to us—not yet anyway.

Most of life is reasonably predictable. The winning numbers in next week's lottery or the winner of next Saturday's race may not be easy to foresee, but most of life follows a predictable pattern. Tomorrow I'll probably get up at the usual time, eat the usual breakfast, go to my usual job, do the usual tasks, meet the usual people. Too much predictability can become boring, so we break it up with the occasional vacation, although even then we often go to the same vacation spot. Because most of life is predictable, we tend to function as if it were certain. But it isn't. The truth is, before you reach the end of this page, an airplane may crash through your roof, or the phone may ring with the message of an unexpected death or the train you are riding in may go off the rails. Each possibility is improbable, within one person's life, but it is exactly that improbability that gives a crisis its stunning psychological impact.

Most of the philosophical reflection that victims engage in is really an attempt to reestablish their old illusion of an ordered existence: "Why did it happen?" "Maybe if I'd gone the other way . . ." "If only I hadn't gone to work that day . . ." Formal inquiries often follow large-scale crises, such as the inquiries after the Waco incident in 1993 and after the Columbine High School shootings in 1999. Sometimes these reflections or investigations lead to practical ways to reduce the future risk of similar crises, but often they are an expression of the mistaken hope that if we can understand

> *Attempts to make sense of the experience are really attempts to regain the illusion that we are in control of our lives.*

what caused a crisis, we can prevent it. The survivors of a crisis don't want to believe that their suffering served no useful purpose at all, so they hope that it can at least provide lessons for the future. Sometimes it can, but often it can't. Attempts to make sense of the experience are really attempts to regain the illusion that we are in control of our lives.

> *During this phase, many victims realize that they have changed, that they will never see life in quite the same way as before.*

Again we want to emphasize the *normality* of all these reactions. Crisis victims were no more self-deluding than the rest of us about their invulnerability, immortality or control over their lives. They just had the bad luck of having those delusions cruelly and suddenly destroyed, leaving them without the psychological shelter that these assumptions usually provide in day-to-day living. A crisis challenges our fundamental assumptions about life and prompts some rethinking. During this phase, many victims realize that *they* have changed, that they will never see life in quite the same way as before. This realization may result in changed life priorities, or sometimes in a complete change in lifestyle or goals.

Laying to rest

As a result of accepting and working through her normal distress reactions, a victim can finally lay her crisis to rest as a bad memory. She can accept that her life has changed because of it, but she can also put it into perspective. Victims are sometimes encouraged to "forget all about it," advice that may be well-intended but is simply impossible. Someone who has worked successfully through the Crisis Response and Recovery Cycle can expect life to toss her occasional reminders of the crisis. Realistically, she should expect to feel bad temporarily, but then she'll be able to say, "Oh well, that's behind me," and get on with life.

This is quite different from the reminders you create for yourself, when nothing outside you has triggered the memory but you have instead brought it to your own mind. This self-initiated mental review of the crisis experience is a normal part of the recovery cycle. It is sometimes a way for the victim to come to terms, in manageable bites, with the reality of what has happened. Allow the painful memories into your mind until the hurt is too much, then turn them off for now, only returning to them later when you feel you can cope with more.

> *Confronting your hurt in bites can make it more manageable than trying to confront it all at once.*

Confronting your hurt in bites can make it more manageable than trying to confront it all at once. But these self-initiated reminders should gradually disappear as you work through the recovery phase. A sign of having laid your crisis to rest would be your ability to cope with the occasional reminders life will throw at you, but not haunting yourself with self-initiated reminders.

Friends and family

As we point out earlier in this chapter, friends and family of a victim can either help or interfere with the victim working through

the cycle, similar to the ways in which the victim can help or
hinder himself. The basic ingredients of a successful recovery are

- Accepting the normality of your stress reactions
  during and after the crisis

- Managing and expressing your feelings constructively

- Eventually coming to terms with what the experience
  has meant and how it has changed you

Any steps you can take to support these processes will aid
your recovery, while any steps you take to block these processes
will hinder your recovery. The same applies to those around you.

Others can be understandably upset by the distress of a victim.
That they want to ease that distress is also understandable.
Unfortunately, these understandable reactions can easily mislead
them into encouraging the victim to deny her normal stress
reactions: "There, there, it's all over now, so you can stop feeling
bad." (If only it were that easy!) If the victim realizes her distress is
disturbing those around her, she may believe she should hide it,
just when she should be expressing it. If others are expressing a lot
of anger toward a possible cause of the crisis, that anger may
further upset the victim and convince her to deny her own anger.

The recovery cycle can take some time, especially after a
severe crisis, and the patience of others can wear thin. This
becomes more likely when the victim displays the extreme mood
swings or active, possibly displaced, anger that are normal
components of recovery but may seem puzzling or unfair to others.
Significant others can help the victim recover if they also receive
counseling about the Crisis Response and Recovery Cycle and
advice about what they can do to help and not hinder the victim's
progress through that cycle.

2

Coping with Personal Disasters

I n this chapter we focus on *personal disasters*, which are
traumatic crises affecting only one victim, or at most a few
victims. A *traumatic crisis* is one that has suddenly caused or
threatened physical harm or significant personal property loss or
damage. Some crises are over quickly, such as an assault on the
street, while others last longer, such as a house fire or being
trapped in a vehicle accident. In this chapter, we discuss the effects
of violent crimes, including sexual assault, torture, robbery,
burglary and accidents. This is *not* an exhaustive list of possible
traumatic crises, but the principles we cover for these more
common traumatic crises can be applied to other, similarly
traumatic experiences.

The Crisis Response and Recovery Cycle (CRRC) and our
suggestions for managing it (see chapter 1) apply directly to
traumatic crises. In fact, much of the research we have used in
writing this book comes from work with the victims of traumatic
crises. The purpose of this chapter is to provide more detailed
descriptions of typical reactions to personal disasters in hope that
these descriptions help victims accept the normality of their own
reactions. When appropriate, we offer extra suggestions that are
relevant to managing a particular type of crisis.

Violent Crime

Dr. Steven Berglas, a clinical psychologist who conducts treatment
programs for crisis victims at McLean Hospital at Harvard Medical

School, has described in detail the reactions to being a victim of violent crime. What he calls the *crisis reaction* is similar to the general pattern of the CRRC, but it is especially relevant to traumatic crises. The crisis reaction includes three distinct stages, although, as we have emphasized, reactions vary for each person depending on the nature of the crime and the makeup of the victim.

Initial impact

The initial impact stage occurs during the hours or days that immediately follow the crime. At this point, a typical victim just is not capable of normal functioning. She experiences shock, disbelief and disorientation that can become physically immobilizing. Many are so paralyzed they are unable to report their experience to police or helping professionals. This is demonstrated clearly by an event that occurred in Melbourne, Australia, at the time we were writing this chapter. A passerby observed an armed holdup taking place in a post office and called the police. When the police arrived, the blinds on the post office windows were closed. Fearing the robber was holding hostages inside, they surrounded the post office for several hours. Eventually the postmaster emerged to say that the robber had long since fled. The staff had been too terrified to move until another postmaster telephoned them to say the police were outside. The reaction of the police, while understandable, was also typical in both its nature and its potential harm to the victims: They told the victims that the first thing they should have done was call the police. While this advice seems logical, it doesn't take into account the paralyzing level of fear many victims experience. Without trying, the police may have added to the victims' self-blame for not handling the situation "better."

Recoil

The next stage observed by Dr. Berglas is the recoil stage, during which victims try to regain their sense of self and some control. For many this involves mentally reviewing the traumatic event through fantasies, dreams or nightmares. This may help release pent-up anger, but it can also be painful and disturbing, especially if a victim remembers a previously repressed experience of extreme horror or humiliation. During this stage most victims experience the extreme mood swings described in the CRRC, fluctuating between feeling competent and helpless, apathetic and angry, resigned and outraged, calm and anxious.

Like crisis victims in general, victims of violent crime mentally review their experience to try to make sense of it. "Why did this happen to me?" However, they are vulnerable to a particular distortion of this question. For many it becomes, "What did I do to deserve this?" Self-blaming is a common reaction among violent-crime victims. Some see their victimization as a result of something bad in their past or present character. Some rape victims exaggerate minor misdeeds in their past to explain why they were attacked.

> *Like crisis victims in general, victims of violent crime mentally review their experience to try to make sense of it.*

A similarly unrealistic perspective creeps into their judgments of their behavior during the crisis: "Why was I so stupid? Why didn't I do [something else] instead?" Some victims cannot accept their panicked, disoriented and ineffective behavior as normal. Deciding that their behavior in response to the crisis was incompetent or stupid, some victims then doubt their ability to deal with the demands of normal living.

> *Deciding that their behavior in response to the crisis was incompetent or stupid, some victims then doubt their ability to deal with the demands of normal living.*

The serious risk in this unfair self-blaming is to your self-esteem. If you do not accept the normality of your reactions during and after your crisis, but instead see them as evidence of your personal shortcomings or weakness, you are judging yourself in an unrealistic way. The result of this self-blaming and self-devaluing, as we explain in chapter 10, is likely to be unnecessary depression and guilt. You are going to feel bad enough about your crisis, without adding extra bad feelings.

You face an important juggling act. As we explain in chapter 1, a crisis experience devastates us because it contradicts our beliefs in a just, fair and predictable world. These beliefs are, in fact, false, but they develop early in life to protect us from the unbearable anxiety we would suffer if we worried constantly about the real but slim possibility that we might be struck down in some way at any moment. To function normally we need to believe that if we do "the right thing," life will in turn be fair to us. In the same vein, we need to be able to trust the people around us.

To function normally we need to believe that if we do "the right thing," life will in turn be fair to us.

Being the victim of a violent crime flatly contradicts these beliefs. Most of the victim's mental review involves an attempt to revive them. Essentially they are thinking, "There must be *some* explanation for why I was a victim and, if I can find it, I can protect myself in the future. I don't have to spend the rest of my life in fear of being a victim again." On the one hand, this natural desire to reduce anxiety by restoring your belief in a safe and fair world can lead you to unfair and unrealistic self-blaming. We advise you against that. Be realistic and therefore fair in judging your own behavior. On the other hand, if you can find a *genuine* way in which you contributed to your crisis, recognizing that and taking practical steps to avoid that risk in the future can help to restore your sense of control.

You don't run the universe, so you can't remove all risk from it, but you are not always a helpless pawn of fate.

You don't run the universe, so you can't remove all risk from it, but you are not always a helpless pawn of fate. Try to look at your behavior before and during your crisis as objectively but as fairly as you can. Don't criticize yourself for your normal human reactions to a crisis, but if you can recognize that in some way you made a real mistake, accept your natural regrets about that and learn from it.

Resolution

Dr. Berglas's third stage is resolution, which is similar to the philosophical reflection and laying-to-rest stages at the end of the CRRC. The best outcome, he says, is for victims to get their crisis experience into perspective so they can use their mental and physical energies elsewhere in their lives. Dr. Berglas warns that even those able to put the crisis into perspective may experience unresolved bad feelings that surface years after the trauma, causing intense anxiety or depression.

These long-term reactions to trauma are similar to the post-traumatic stress disorders (PTSD) seen in soldiers after intense military combat. Sufferers of PTSD experience chronic anxiety, difficulty concentrating, memory loss, guilty feelings and sleep disturbances. Many also have trouble establishing successful relationships or may withdraw from existing relationships. Although this self-imposed isolation may protect a victim from having to cope with feelings of mistrust, it also cuts him off from potential social support, just when that support could be vital.

Severity of reaction—five factors

Drs. Diana and Louis Everstine (who have worked extensively with violent-crime victims) have identified a number of factors that influence the severity of the emotional disturbance caused by a violent crime.

First is the degree to which the victim's body was violated. Assaults in which the body was penetrated in some way, such as shootings, stabbings and rape, are usually more traumatic than those not resulting in injury. But even property loss or damage as a result of a burglary causes psychological stress, because our home and our possessions are psychological extensions of ourselves.

Second is how much the victim feared that she was going to be killed.

Third is the relationship between the victim and the attacker. An attack by someone known to the victim is usually more traumatic than one committed by a stranger, presumably because it represents a violation of trust.

Fourth is the location of the incident. An attack in a place where the victim felt safe and secure, such as at home or work, is usually more traumatic than one occurring in a public place. This same sense of violation of a safe and private place occurs after burglary, even when you weren't present at the time of the incident.

The fifth factor, as you might expect, involves the victim's past experiences and present coping skills. These influence the degree of psychological trauma caused by the present incident.

Effects of Violent Crime on Female Victims

	Possible Effects		
	---	---	---
	Had nervous breakdown	Thought seriously of suicide	Attempted suicide
	percent	percent	percent
Nonvictims	3.3	6.8	2.2
Victims of			
attempted rape	8.9	29.1	8.9
completed rape	16.0	44.0	19.0
attempted sexual molestation	5.4	32.4	8.1
completed sexual molestation	1.8	21.8	3.6
attempted robbery	0.0	9.1	12.1
completed robbery	7.7	10.8	3.1
aggravated assault	2.1	14.9	4.3

Psychologist Dean Kilpatrick and his colleagues at the Medical University of South Carolina have researched the psychological consequences for women of being the victim of different kinds of violent crime. Their results are in the table above.

As you would expect, women victims in general suffered more psychological problems than women who had not been victims. For example, only 2.2 percent of nonvictims had attempted suicide compared with 19 percent of rape victims or even 4.3 percent of assault victims. Sex crimes, especially rape, caused the most serious consequences. A finding that at first seems strange is that *attempted* sexual molestation and *attempted* robbery had more serious consequences than the completed crimes. The researchers concluded that this was because the incomplete crimes left the victims imagining what might have happened, whereas the victims of completed crimes knew the worst already.

We have reviewed these factors not to suggest that you should be feeling worse than you might be, but to help you understand that even the most intense reactions to being the victim of a violent crime fall within the normal range of human behavior. As we mention in chapter 1, some of the people around you may give you the opposite impression, that your reactions are abnormal, either out of misguided helpfulness or as a result of their own inability to cope with what has happened to you.

Nonvictims and violent crime

However helpful their intentions, people who tell you in various ways to "forget it" are simply being unrealistic. They are demonstrating their own ignorance about the normal human reactions to crisis and about the best way to work through those reactions. We suggest that you show you appreciate their intentions but give them feedback on how unhelpful they actually are and what you would like instead. For example, "I appreciate your trying to help me cope, but when you tell me just to forget such a bad experience, you're suggesting something impossible. It discourages me from telling you how I really feel and that makes me feel even more isolated. I would find it more helpful if you would just show you understand and accept how I'm feeling right now."

> ## "Forget about it?"
>
> When well-meaning friends and family encourage you to forget
> your experience, you can let them know how unrealistic that
> is without stepping on any toes. Show you appreciate their
> intentions but then give them feedback on how unhelpful they
> actually are and what you would like instead.
>
> "I appreciate your trying to help me cope, but when you tell
> me just to forget such a bad experience, you're suggesting
> something impossible. It discourages me from telling you how
> I really feel and that makes me feel even more isolated. I would
> find it more helpful if you would just show you understand
> and accept how I'm feeling right now."

Some experts believe there is another reason why nonvictims
are unhelpful to victims. Nonvictims, like victims, need to believe
in a safe, predictable and fair world in order to be able to function
normally themselves. Sociologist Erving Goffman has said that
victims of crime, disease or disaster often arouse extremely
negative feelings in nonvictims because they make nonvictims feel
vulnerable to similar crises. To protect
themselves from the fear that
a similar crisis could happen to them,
nonvictims may try to blame the victim,
at least partly, for his crisis experience:
"He should have known better than to
be in that part of town
at that time of night." "She was really
asking for it, going to a place like that
alone." Reactions like these, however understandable, put an
emotional barrier between the victim and those around her.

Victims of crime, disease or disaster often arouse extremely negative feelings in nonvictims because they make nonvictims feel vulnerable to similar crises.

A similar process sometimes happens when the victim is
receiving professional help. Professional helpers, whether they
are emergency personnel such as police, firefighters or rescuers,
or health and support personnel such as doctors, nurses,
psychologists or counselors, are also faced with a heavy emotional

burden when confronted by victims. This burden is further increased if the case is even more horrific than usual or a large-scale disaster. To protect themselves and to help them cope with their vital tasks, some professional helpers adopt a detached and businesslike approach. Again this is an understandable reaction on their part, but victims may see it as an uncaring rejection by the people who are supposed to be helping them.

Nonvictims may also avoid victims for another understandable reason. Camille Wortman, a social psychologist at the University of Michigan, has found that nonvictims may avoid victims because they are afraid they won't be able to help. Just as few of us are ever prepared for being victims of crises, few of us are prepared to be helpful nonvictims, to offer effective emotional support to victims. Confronted with an obviously distressed victim, many nonvictims feel incompetent just because they are unable to take away the victim's distress.

> *Nonvictims may avoid victims because they are afraid they won't be able to help.*

The practical implication of these observations is the need for nonvictims, whether professional helpers or friends, family or total strangers, to set realistic goals. *Nothing* is going to lessen a victim's distress quickly or easily and attempts to postpone it usually make it worse in the long run. The most helpful support nonvictims can provide is to show clearly that they understand and accept the victim's distress. Then the victim in turn can do the same and begin working through a healthy crisis response and recovery. The communication skills for providing this support are spelled out later in the book, especially in chapter 8. This is a much more emotionally demanding task for nonvictims than protecting their own feelings by encouraging a victim to deny his. Nonvictims have to decide whether they are involved with the victim for his benefit or their own.

Rape

Our discussion above of the effects of violent crime clearly applies to rape and should be read by rape victims or those trying to help them. Rape, however, needs further consideration. As the figures on page 18 show, rape is the violent crime that has the most devastating psychological effects on its victims. These victims are usually women, although there is evidence that the number of men victims of rape (by other men) is increasing, and it is also possible that the victim may be a child. We focus here on the more common situation of a woman being the victim of rape, but the principles can be applied to other victims.

Because of its sexual component, rape has often been misrepresented, especially by defense lawyers and chauvinists, and misunderstood, especially by nonvictims. Rape is not a sexual encounter in any usual sense. It is an assault in which the rapist attempts to hurt his victim by means of sex. Although the rapist is usually sexually aroused when committing rape, his main motivation is to hurt the victim. In fact, some rapists do not become sexually aroused until after they have hurt or humiliated their victims. The other disturbing by-product of this primarily aggressive motivation for rape is that habitual rapists tend to become increasingly violent from one rape to the next. This has a practical implication when a victim has doubts about reporting her rape to the authorities.

For their part, rape victims do not become sexually aroused. The widespread belief that women need and even enjoy being coaxed into sex, perhaps forcibly, reflects the tragic absence of honest human-relations education in schools and homes. This results in an undue and uncritical acceptance of jokes as a source of information, many of those jokes expressing and reinforcing the sexism that is still strong in our culture. None of the research we have ever seen includes even a single report of a rape victim enjoying any part of her experience. Rape victims feel terrified and humiliated and they experience pain, sometimes serious injury or death. We begin by making these points about the real nature of rape because popular misunderstandings about it often increase the suffering of victims.

Rape is assault.

Rape is assault. All rapes involve force, either threatened or actual. In most cases, the psychological wounds are worse and will be felt longer than the physical ones. Because they are psychological and therefore "invisible," they are harder for victims and nonvictims to understand and to heal.

People usually have a "private space" around them, a circle about two feet across. The size of this private space varies in different cultures, but it's there. Consider how uncomfortable you feel when someone invades your private space by coming too close without being invited by you. A rape victim has suffered the ultimate violation of this psychological territory because not only

> *Being raped destroys the victim's basic sense of trust in others.*

her private space but her body has been invaded. This may destroy her sense of integrity, of wholeness. Victims of robbery or burglary experience a similar sense of territorial violation, but it is a thousand times worse for a rape victim.

Being raped destroys the victim's basic sense of trust in others. This destruction of trust is more extreme when the attacker is someone the victim knows, as is often but not always the case. Rebuilding trust in others can be one of the most difficult parts of recovery for a rape victim.

She may also lose trust in herself. Most of us believe that if we say "No!" to someone, then he will stop whatever it is we don't like, even if we have to repeat ourselves. A rape victim has this belief shattered and the resulting feeling of powerlessness can cause her to doubt her competence in dealing with other people and in controlling her life.

> *To salvage our belief in a just and fair world, we search for a just and fair reason for our victimization.*

Rape victims, like other crisis victims, have a strong need to find an explanation for their experience. Unfortunately, as for victims of other assaults, "Why me?" too often becomes "What did I do wrong? What did I do to deserve this?" To salvage our belief in a just and fair world, we search for a just and fair reason for our victimization. In one case, an adolescent girl was taken to a counselor by her parents because of her unusual behavior. She only reluctantly reported that she had been raped, and she would not cooperate with the police, even though she had told her parents she knew what her attacker looked like. Only after she had begun therapy did it emerge that she believed her rape was God's punishment for her previous misbehavior as a teenager. Once she stated this belief, her therapist was able to help her question it and work through to a full recovery.

Many rape victims also blame themselves afterward for not fighting their attacker or trying to escape. Like other crisis victims, they are critical of their own behavior during the crisis. They need to understand that they were in shock and that the normal human response during a crisis that lasts longer than a few seconds is the frozen survival state. A rape, or other violent assault, is not the kind of experience during which you can realistically expect to think clearly or act cleverly. For most victims it is an experience of terror during which their primary goal is to survive. This overwhelming focus on survival may lead a victim to comply with the rapist's demands, which are often intended to degrade and humiliate the victim. Later a victim may feel intense distress remembering parts of her own behavior. That's a normal stress reaction. But it is unfair and unrealistic to judge your survival behavior negatively, instead of accepting it as an adaptive response to a horrible situation.

Another part of the normal, self-protective reaction to a crisis, especially one as severe as a rape, is to block out some of the ugliest memories. Some of them may never come back. Some may return at different times during recovery. This is the mind's way of trying to limit how much it has to deal with at any one time. It does not mean that a victim with blank spots in her memory is suffering from anything unusual. If returning memories disturb you, we suggest the techniques in chapter 8.

If returning memories disturb you, we suggest the techniques in chapter 8.

Some rape victims fall into the trap of trying to deny their bad feelings, for two reasons: First, admitting how bad they feel is like admitting to their attacker, even in his absence, how much he has hurt them. Second, some don't want to disturb family or friends, especially husbands or boyfriends. However understandable these victim's concerns are, she needs to accept that her successful recovery begins with accepting her bad feelings as normal reactions to her experience.

A rape victim's needs are almost contradictory.

Many rape victims are plagued by fears of another attack, even when the rapist has been imprisoned. These fears are understandably worse if he has not been arrested, or if he avoids imprisonment. To cope with these fears, the victim should take reasonable precautions to ensure her personal safety, without exaggerating the fears any further. For example, there are self-defense courses run specifically for women. Taking one of these courses can help a woman see herself as less at risk and more capable of defending herself and escaping from any future assault. Some of these programs teach women to think defensively, which means learning to avoid high-risk situations. All of these lessons can help restore some of her self-confidence and diminish her sense of powerlessness. The police and several crime-prevention programs offer advice on how to make your home more secure, with appropriate locks and similar steps. A night light, a handy flashlight, leaving the radio on, getting a dog, any simple step that increases your sense of safety is worth trying. None of these steps is sufficient alone, and sadly none of them *guarantees* your future safety, but taking them can reduce your feeling of being a helpless victim.

Nonvictims and rape

Because rape can be the most psychologically disturbing violent crime, the people around a rape victim have a more crucial role to play than those around a victim of other violent crimes. A rape victim's needs are almost contradictory: On the one hand, she needs a great deal of support and sympathetic direction, but on the other hand, she needs to set her own pace for recovery so that her experience of powerlessness is not reinforced. Family and friends need supportive information or counseling if they are to play a helpful role. For example, when some rape victims begin to experience the normal anger of the recovery phase, they have a lot of trouble expressing it toward the rapist, perhaps because they fear another attack. The victim may displace the anger onto others, including a husband, boyfriend or father. It's also possible that an element of this anger is resentment at a man whom she sees as a "failed protector." Some victims feel anger toward any man, at least for a while. In any case, both victim and nonvictims need to use skills like those described in chapters 9 and 10 to handle this normal part of the recovery cycle without unnecessary damage.

One researcher reported the sad finding that in about half of all rape cases, the victim's primary love relationship or marriage ended after, and at least partly as a result of, the rape. In some cases, the rape would have magnified existing problems in a relationship, just as it can interact with individual problems a woman was suffering before she was raped. But in some cases, the rape caused an unnecessary end to a relationship and robbed the woman of valuable support because of a lack of appropriate advice for both the victim and the nonvictims around her.

Rape and the law

Researchers generally agree that many and possibly most rapes go unreported. We have already explained some of the factors that might lead a woman to conceal her experience, at least from the authorities. The prejudiced and sometimes aggressive reactions of police, courts and society in general are further discouragement. This situation has been improving because of more accurate public information and the action of some women's groups. Today, police usually have specially trained personnel who handle rape cases more sensitively than used to be the case. Laws have mostly been changed to recognize that rape is a crime of violent assault and to offer more protection for the feelings and privacy of victims.

Nonetheless, reporting a rape and following through the legal process is still an additional source of stress, sometimes quite severe, inflicted on a victim whose reserves are already drained. We recognize this, but we still want to encourage victims to report their rapes to police, even though this can be difficult. There are strong reasons for reporting:

1. It is unlikely that a rapist will rape only once. Most will commit a series of rapes, some with increasing violence, until they are stopped. Even if one victim's report does not result in an arrest or conviction, it can become part of a growing pattern of information that eventually leads to an arrest and successful conviction.

2. Knowing of her attacker's arrest and conviction can help a victim recover and regain some sense of an ordered life.

3. Even if her report does not lead to an arrest, or if the charged man escapes conviction, she can still have the satisfaction of knowing she did what she could to right the wrong done to her, that she fought back as a responsible citizen does, with the law as her weapon.

Following through the legal process, from medical examination through interviews and attempts at identification to giving evidence in court, will be a further source of stress. We strongly suggest you get support for this. Sexual assault centers and some women's groups can put you in touch with other victims and offer a level of support and understanding not available from other sources. (See the Resources section on page 215.) They can also help you to prepare yourself for each step in the legal process. Or consider some other counseling or therapy, if you prefer. Just don't tough it out alone.

Most rape victims say they want family, including husbands or boyfriends, nearby but not necessarily present during this process. For some situations, such as an identification parade or giving evidence in court, the presence of a husband, lover or parent may be an added stress for the victim. These significant others may also find the victim's distress difficult to handle constructively. The victim is her own best judge of what is most helpful from others, and she should be assertive enough to ask for it. Nonvictims should try to understand the victim's mixture of feelings during this prolonged reminder of her experience and be willing to offer help without forcing the issue.

The high failure rate of victims' relationships after rape underlines the important role of husbands and lovers, who are indirect but real victims themselves. They need to debunk popular misconceptions about rape in their own thinking, while accepting the understandable anger they may feel toward the victim for not having been "more careful." These close nonvictims need to look beyond the sexual component of the rape to understand its full effects on the victim, as we have been describing them above. They need to realize the victim will need broad and ongoing support to recover from her physical assault, and to regain her sense of integrity and personal worth.

A difficult issue is the question of resuming sexual relations. A well-intended attempt to show the victim she is still loved and

> *A well-intended attempt to show the victim she is still loved and wanted may be perceived by her as frightening pressure.*

wanted may be perceived by her as frightening pressure. Keeping too aloof out of fear of doing the wrong thing may be seen as rejection. There really is no substitute for good, plain, honest and open communication. For example, "I want you to know that I am looking forward to making love with you again, when you feel ready for it. But I also don't want to put any pressure on you because I realize what a horrible experience you had. So I would like you to let me know when you feel ready." In a good relationship, people can share physical affection, which can be supportive, without it having to lead to sex, unless both partners want that. When you are invited to resume your sexual relationship, a gentle and sensitive approach is obviously the way to go.

We mention earlier that sometimes children are the victims of rape or other sexual assaults. When the perpetrator is a stranger to the child victim, the principles we outline above apply and we hope that parents find them helpful, although many parents will find supportive counseling helpful as well. The sad truth, however, is that the adult who sexually assaults a child is much more likely to be someone the child knows, often a family member, than a stranger. For this reason, we consider the effects of sexual assault on children in more detail in chapter 4.

Prolonged Terror

Most personal disasters, such as violent crimes, robberies and rapes, are over in a relatively short time. However, sometimes a robbery or rape may be prolonged, as incidents of kidnapping and hostage-taking often are. In addition to all the points discussed so far, the particular effects of an experience of prolonged terror requires further consideration.

In most cases of people being attacked or held captive, there is little real chance of escape. This is as true of prolonged crises as brief ones. Few victims are capable of overpowering their attackers, lacking either the strength or weapons to do so. Furthermore, the normal reaction is to go into shock and the frozen survival state, with an understandable focus on personal survival. During a prolonged crisis these normal reactions can interact with the restricted nature of the situation to make a victim identify with his captor or captors; some even form an emotional attachment.

This is known as the *Stockholm syndrome* because it was first studied closely after a prolonged hostage-holding incident in Stockholm, Sweden. It is hard for nonvictims to understand, and victims may judge themselves harshly afterward, especially if they actively assisted their captors. You need to consider the situation *as it is experienced by the victim*.

> *You need to consider the situation as it is experienced by the victim.*

She is usually in direct contact with only her captor, and possibly other victims, so there is no one else to relate to. She is probably getting information about what is happening only from her captor, who will inevitably give that information his own slant: "See how the police don't care what happens to you, or they would have

In the victim's view, the captor becomes the person who allows the victim to live.

accepted my demands by now." In the victim's view, the captor becomes the person who allows the victim to live, who "protects" her while her employer or family or the police and wider community have "failed" to protect her. This may not make much sense in the cool light of day, but to a shocked and terrified victim kept in a situation that seems drawn out by the actions of the authorities dealing with her captors, it can seem quite plausible. In some cases the captors show the same distress as their victims, further increasing the likelihood of a bond forming.

One of the best known examples of the Stockholm syndrome involved Patty Hearst, the American heiress. So complete was her identification with her kidnappers after being held for some time that she joined them in a bank raid during which she was filmed by a bank security camera. At her subsequent trial she reported the same extreme disorientation of prolonged victimization that predictably met with public skepticism. However, it has been found that this remarkable change in how the victim perceives her captor can take place within a few hours. It is more likely to occur if there have been clear threats to the victim, if the victim believes the captor has spared her life or if the victim believes the captor is the only person who can now save her.

It is easy to be smart after any event.

Victims and nonvictims need to understand exactly how the crisis situation has affected the thinking and perceptions of the victim at the time, taking into *realistic* account the effects of shock and the normal focus on personal survival that occurs during the frozen survival state. It is easy to be smart *after* any event. It is human to react to personal disasters, including prolonged ones, in the ways we are describing.

Torture

Fortunately, torture is a rare event in North America, the result of unusual crimes rather than the instrument of government policy that it is in some countries. However, a surprising number of torture victims live in our community, as a result of escaping or migrating from their own. Amnesty International lists 125 countries in which torture is practiced today. According to the U.S. Center for Victims of Torture, the United States accepts refugees from 45 countries, and about 25 percent of these refugees were victims of torture.

Torture victims show many of the symptoms of the post-traumatic stress disorder seen in victims of combat and large-scale disasters, but in a more severe form. Torture's unique characteristic is that physical pain is being inflicted, usually over a prolonged period, by someone whose clear intention is to destroy the victim totally, psychologically as well as physically. Afterward, victims must cope with both physical and psychological scars. The situation can be complicated by the torture victims' mistrust of government authorities, an understandable reaction to their experiences in their old country but a barrier to their seeking assistance in their new country. On top of everything, they may suffer the dislocation and isolation felt by most immigrants in a new country and a foreign culture.

The treatment of the effects of torture is such a comparatively new discipline, and the effects are so severe, that this really falls outside the bounds of self-help. Several support programs for torture victims exist in the United States and Canada (see the Resources section on page 215). We encourage torture victims and those close to them to seek professional help.

Accidents

Easily one of the most common traumatic crises is to be the victim of an accident, on the road, during some kind of recreation, at work or wherever. The CRRC is an appropriate description of the way people usually react to being accident victims, and the suggestions in chapters 7 through 11 provide a step-by-step plan for recovering from the psychological disturbance caused by an accident.

However, the word "accident" is sometimes inappropriately used to imply that the event in question happened entirely by *chance*, that it was unforeseeable and unpreventable. In fact, some accidents are caused, at least partly, by human error or negligence. There may have been an element of chance or bad luck, but there is also an element of fault. In the United States, in fact, the term "car accident" has been replaced by "car crash" for exactly this reason. For example, many accidents, in recreation and at work as well as on the roads, involve alcohol consumption. The probability that someone is personally responsible may affect victims in additional ways.

Accident victims who can legitimately blame someone else, at least in part, for what happened to them may benefit from having an appropriate target for their anger. Being able to find a plausible explanation for what caused their accident can help to restore some of their lost sense of safety, especially if it prompts constructive action to reduce similar risks in the future. On the other hand, if the accident leads to a drawn-out attempt to seek some kind of payback, such as a lawsuit or compensation case, then the suffering will also be drawn out and recovery delayed. If the victims do not reach an outcome that is fair and just, then that will probably add to their distress even more.

On the other side of the experience, some people will have to come to grips with the fact that they caused or contributed to an accident. They may even have escaped injury themselves, but they will nonetheless be psychological victims. Clearly the most likely psychological consequences of their crisis experiences are guilt and depression. Chapters 8 and 10 contain our best suggestions for coping with this kind of personal disaster.

3

Coping with Death and Grief

W e've all heard some form of this old saying: Only two things in life are certain—death and taxes. The success of some tax dodgers suggests that taxation may not be so inevitable, at least for those with a small social conscience and creative accountants. But death remains the life crisis we will all have to face—the death of those close to us and our own deaths. In this chapter we discuss both of these life crises: facing your own death and coping with your grief over someone else's.

Religion, especially formal religion, plays a much smaller role in our community and in most people's lives than it used to. People turn to religion, at least for formal ceremony and consolation, most often when facing the death of a loved one. If you have religious beliefs or if you seek support from a religious counselor, such as a minister, priest or rabbi, and you find that helpful, then we encourage you to continue. We do not discuss religious issues in this chapter because, as psychologists, we have no expertise in religion. We restrict ourselves to those topics we can claim special training in, and we offer you psychological advice for coping with death and grief.

There is no doubt that many people obtain worthwhile support from their religious beliefs throughout their lives. Many Christians, Jews, Muslims, Buddhists and others hold views of life and death that help them accept their own deaths with serenity and see a positive side to the loss of someone else. We emphasize that not considering religious issues in this book is not meant as a criticism of taking a religious approach. We simply do not pretend to be experts in a field we are not and do not wish to attack people's rights to their own beliefs. We do not hold religious beliefs nor practice a religion ourselves. That's our choice. If you do hold religious beliefs and you find them helpful, stick with your choice. If you want more religious support for coping with death or grief, we encourage you to talk with your own religious counselor. Meanwhile, let us offer you psychological support.

Your Own Death

Let's get our goals straight and realistic. We are not really talking about coping with death, because there is nothing there to cope with. Once you are dead, there is no "you" that needs to cope with anything. Death returns us to the state of biological and psychological non-existence that applied before our lives began. In that state, we do not exist to experience anything at all, so there is nothing to cope with. (As we said above, we are not considering the issue of a spiritual existence after death because it falls outside our area of professional knowledge.)

Living with dying

The crisis most of us have to face, sooner or later, is *dying*, not death. Living with the expectation that we are going to die is the real crisis. In principle this could apply to all of us, all of the time. You can dodge the tax man but not the grim reaper. As we discuss in the first chapter, most of us cope with the eventual certainty of our own death by disregarding it: "Sure, I know I'm going to die, but not now, and not in the foreseeable future." This self-delusion makes life under the shadow of inevitable death workable. The shattering of this delusion is what gives many crises their disturbing impact.

> *Living with the expectation that we are going to die is the real crisis.*

For some, death comes during sleep or unconsciousness or so quickly that they aren't aware of its approach. Some crises are so traumatic and brief that a person has time only for the crisis response. Victims may experience terror or pain, then shock and the frozen survival state, but they may not have much opportunity to cope with impending death. Some survivors of these traumatic, life-threatening crises report that their lives flashed before their eyes, while others tried to make some quick preparation for death. For example, one passenger on British Airways Flight 009, which lost all engine power for twelve minutes after flying into a cloud of volcanic dust in 1982, wrote a brief message to his wife on his ticket. He wrapped it with his passport in a plastic bag, in the hope it would be found and given to her. Another passenger kicked off his boots and took out a penknife to fight off sharks, in case the plane crashed in the sea. Most of the passengers did not even make such simple preparations, so high was their stress and so brief was the warning of possible death.

For many people death is signaled, with more or less certainty, far enough ahead of its occurrence to create the crisis of coping with dying. The most likely situation is to be told you have a life-threatening illness, although just growing old can prompt a similar reaction in some people. Dr. Avery Weisman has researched people's reactions to being told they have a life-threatening illness and his observations of their reactions fit within the Crisis Response and Recovery Cycle (CRRC), including the fact that individuals naturally vary in how each of them reacts.

Many people react to the news that they have a life-threatening illness with denial, sometimes expressed in terms of hope for a postponement of death. Some become angry at their fate, or at what they see as the failure of people or systems that were supposed to protect them. Many engage in the philosophical review that is common in the CRRC, and some change priorities and values. Ideally, a complete recovery cycle would result in a realistic and resigned acceptance of death, if it must come, without unnecessary distress. Dr. Weisman suggests that an appropriate death is to die as you would choose, if you have to and can make that choice.

The major risk in not coping with the crisis of your approaching death is that your natural anxiety and depression will be exaggerated and will block your realistic goal of living as well as you can, right to the end. Dr. Wendy Sobel, a clinical psychologist at Boston College, has identified a number of factors that might make you feel worse than you need to, given that most of us are going to feel bad about dying anyway.

First, you may have to cope with a chronic illness. You may suffer pain or other unpleasant symptoms, as well as medical tests or treatments that can be unpleasant themselves, no matter how necessary they are. Long-term illness and long-term treatment can be physically and psychologically draining. This experience may lead you to feel as if you are losing control of your life, surrendering it to others and becoming helpless. Thoughts like these will increase your depression.

Second, your self-esteem may take a pounding if you blame yourself for being ill or not coping better, both unfair judgments. Dr. Weisman found that some of his patients even saw their approaching deaths as punishment for acts committed years before, adding a dose of guilt to their depression. On top of this, any visible effects of your illness or treatment might make you feel even worse about yourself.

Third, a life-threatening illness or its treatment may interfere with your activities, especially the ones you find rewarding and enjoyable. You may have to give up work or pastimes that were important to you. Such a loss of daily rewards is likely to contribute to depression.

You may have to cope with negative reactions from other people in your life.

Fourth, you may have to cope with negative reactions from other people in your life. Just as you experience a range of normal reactions to your death, so do others in your life. As we discussed in the previous chapter, victims make nonvictims feel uncomfortable, partly because they remind them of their own vulnerability and partly because they make them feel incompetent, unable to help. Some of them will react, unfortunately but understandably, by showing their discomfort or by withdrawing. You could misinterpret their reactions in personally negative ways that will add to your depression.

Coping to the end
Your realistic goal is to make the most of what life is left to you and to prepare yourself to die as you would choose, if you have to. Let us offer you a few suggestions.

Watch your self-talk
How you feel about anything, including your approaching death, is influenced by how you think about it. Those with strong religious beliefs might see death as a gateway to a welcome state of some kind. Those suffering a painful illness might see death as a welcome release. Most of us, however, have some reasonable bad feelings about death. Our only choice is how bad, and how much we let those natural bad feelings intrude into our remaining life.

How you feel about anything, including your approaching death, is influenced by how you think about it.

We strongly suggest you make a deliberate and persistent effort to use the techniques described in chapters 8, 9 and 10, so that you manage and share your bad feelings as effectively as you can. You will help yourself significantly, and those around you. Each of us will have to come to terms with death in our own way and decide what is an appropriate death for us, but consider this coping statement for ideas:

"I expect to feel sad about my approaching death because I will lose relationships and activities that are important to me. I won't deny my sadness or other bad feelings about dying because they're a natural reaction. But I'm not going to let those bad feelings interfere with the rest of my life any more than they have to, by exaggerating them. I'll take whatever constructive and sensible steps I can to postpone my death comfortably, but that's as much as I can do about that. Meanwhile, knowing my life is limited, I intend to make the rest of it as good as I can, for my own sake and for those around me."

Plan and do something constructive to achieve the goal of living as well as you can until you die. Following are further suggestions.

Manage your illness sensibly

As a common-sense rule of thumb, follow the advice of your medical practitioner about treatment, medication, lifestyle and so on. Self-help groups for some chronic illnesses provide important support for both victims and their families. See the Resources section on page 215 for a list of useful organizations or ask your doctor for advice. Don't underestimate how helpful such a group can be. For some illnesses, chronic pain becomes a potential source of distress and depression, so we have outlined a pain-management program below.

We suggest you consider alternative approaches to managing your illness with a degree of caution. The helpfulness of alternative therapies is too large and controversial a topic for us to discuss in detail here. As practicing applied scientists ourselves, we naturally have our own views that tend to be conservative and pragmatic. We have no doubt that some of the ideas put forth by alternative therapists will turn out to be genuinely helpful, especially some of those drawn from the traditional medicines of other cultures. We also have no doubt that some of those ideas are nonsense, sometimes pushed by sincere believers, sometimes pushed by dishonest people who are out to make a buck on other people's pain. The difficulty is deciding which is which, an important question that we can only see being definitively answered by painstaking scientific research. The wrong choice of alternative therapies may give you false hopes and then greater disappointment, may interfere with your mainstream medical treatment or may even be dangerous in itself.

On the other hand, we sympathize with the strong wish for a cure that anyone faced with a life-threatening illness would feel. It is important to maintain as much of your sense of control as you can, by asking to have your illness and treatment explained to you and by taking as much responsibility as you can for managing both. As a part of taking an active role in your self-care, you might understandably want to explore alternatives to your present treatment. Our best suggestion is to do so with caution, *in addition* to your regular treatment, not in place of it. We would think twice if an alternative therapist told us that we should stop our orthodox medical treatment, or could not offer a plausible explanation for why her treatment should be helpful, preferably backed up by independent evidence. We'd also be wary of extreme claims about "miracle cures" or treatments that cost a lot of money.

A strong and growing body of evidence shows that stress interferes with your body's immune response, its ability to protect itself against disease. This includes research findings such as a reduced ability of your body under high and uncontrollable stress to protect itself against cancer. Unfortunately, at the time of writing this book, that's as far as the research goes. It seems reasonably certain that stress management should help to prevent the occurrence of cancer, and reasonably likely that stress management may help to control, perhaps even cure, cancer. But those possibilities have not yet been demonstrated in scientific research despite some of the claims you may run across.

> *Strengthening your ability to manage stress will help you cope with the immediate stress of facing death.*

You have nothing to lose by learning stress-management techniques, and in a way this entire book is a specialized stress-management program. Strengthening your ability to manage stress will help you cope with the immediate stress of facing death. If it also helps you to manage, perhaps even cure, a life-threatening disease, then that's even better!

Keep up the rewards

As we explain in chapter 10, we need two kinds of rewards from life to function well and to avoid unnecessary depression. We need both fun and achievement. Within any limitations imposed by your illness, try to keep up your rewarding activities. If you have to stop some, try to replace them with others. This may be difficult, but it is important, not only for its lifting effect on your mood, but also as a boost for your self-esteem. In chapter 10 we give step-by-step instructions for assessing and rebuilding your rewarding activities.

Nurture your important relationships

Just as you are facing your crisis of approaching death, the important people in your life are facing their crisis of losing you. So everybody is under some stress right now. The problem is that your relationships are going to be more important for offering mutual support at the same time as the strain of those crises can block that support, to everyone's loss. You must communicate. Share information by sharing this chapter or one of the self-help books that focuses on death

Just as you are facing your crisis of approaching death, the important people in your life are facing their crisis of losing you.

and dying. Share feelings, using the skills in chapter 9. Clear the air by making it clear that your illness and death are open to conversation, but that they don't have to be the only thing you talk about. There is more in your life, even now, than just dying. Now is also the time to complete any unfinished business, not only in the technical sense of making sure your will and personal affairs are wrapped up, but in an emotional sense of saying things you may have postponed but know you should say.

There is more in your life, even now, than just dying.

Elizabeth Kübler-Ross has called death the final stage of growth. By accepting your mortality, by accepting the normality of your feelings about your death, by managing those feelings so that you live as well as you can right to the end, and by sharing your feelings so that you and the important people in your life can support each other, you will be working toward giving yourself the death that is appropriate for you. None of us can aim for better than that.

Managing chronic pain

All pain has a psychological component, no matter what is causing it. Many people misunderstand this and think we're saying they are imagining their pain, because they believe if something is "psychological" it is less real than if it is "biological." This belief, however common, reflects a lack of understanding of psychology. Try to imagine a human who does not think or feel or have emotions or motivations. Isn't very human, is she? Our psychology, our inner and outer behavior, is as much a part of being human as our biology is, and it is no less real. The fact that we cannot directly see our inner behavior can make it hard to study, just as it is difficult for physicists to study subatomic particles, but imaginative researchers have found clever scientific ways around that problem. Your psychology is as real as any other aspect of you.

Researchers have concluded that pain has three psychological components. Understanding each gives you three approaches to managing the psychological part of your pain. We assume that, with the help of your medical advisers and some common sense, you are already doing all you can to manage the physical component of your pain. Keep it up, although as you learn to manage the psychological part of your pain, you may need less physical support, such as pain-killing drugs. The three psychological components of pain are the sensory, the emotional and the thinking components.

The *sensory component* involves your perception of the pain, including being aware of and paying attention to it. The *emotional component* includes how you feel about and during pain. The *thinking component* involves how you are thinking about pain and your response to it. As a simple contrast, if you concentrate on your pain, feel tense and anxious about it, and tell yourself you just can't cope anymore, you will probably experience a lot of pain. On the other hand, if you don't notice your pain much, if you feel relaxed and in control and tell yourself you can manage your pain, you will probably experience less of it. Because of your life-threatening illness, you are probably stuck with some pain. But you can exert a lot of control over how much, how intense and how much it interferes with your life. Here are a few suggestions based on the program worked out by psychologists Professor Donald Meichenbaum and Dr. Dennis Turk, at the University of Waterloo in Ontario, Canada.

To reduce the sensory impact of pain, learn *deep muscular relaxation techniques*. Researchers have found that all of the various methods—yoga, biofeedback, progressive training, autogenic imagery and so on—work about equally well, so try one that appeals to you. You may want to join a relaxation class, or teach yourself using a cassette program. While you are relaxing, try to focus your attention on slow, deep breathing. This helps you to relax more and reduces your awareness of the pain.

Try to divert your attention to something other than the pain.

Try to divert your attention to something other than the pain. This means you need easy access to activities that hold your attention, as we discuss in chapter 7 as part of a general coping strategy. Or you can focus on some aspect of your bodily functions, perhaps even the pain itself, but in a detached and clinical way, as something to be studied but not really affecting you directly. Use your imagination by building a fantasy that excludes the pain, such as being somewhere pleasant in a relaxed and comfortable state. Another way to use your imagination is to change, in your mind, the nature or severity of your pain. For example, some people can acknowledge their pain but imagine it as a buzz or a tingle. If you have suffered from pain for long, you have probably worked out some pain-management ideas yourself. *Use your own successful strategies*. Try out all of our suggestions, thoroughly, finding the ones that work for you. Build up your personal set of pain-management techniques.

Finally, try to replace negative self-talk with coping statements. You will learn more about this technique in chapter 8, and it will help you manage the thinking component of pain. Most people's pain comes or peaks at regular times, so you can use different coping statements to prepare yourself for the next episode of pain, to confront it, to manage the peaks and to relax after it's over. See the box on page 44 for examples of effective coping statements. As we explain in chapter 8, you will get the most benefit from these coping statements if you consciously stop yourself from thinking negatively and use these thoughts instead.

There is more to pain management than we have room for in this book, but we can warn you of the four common traps chronic pain sufferers can fall into:

- The *medication trap* involves becoming dependent on pain-killing drugs. Your tolerance to a drug may build until it no longer helps you, even at high doses, or the drug may have unwanted side effects.

- The *take-it-easy trap* can lead to a loss of rewarding activities and a weakening of muscles, which then aggravates pain when you do try something active.

- The *depression trap* involves a cycle of fewer activities giving fewer rewards, which leads to more depression, which triggers a further reduction in activity and so on.

- The *complaint-resentment-guilt trap* occurs when pain has become the focus of your life and your conversation so that you complain, others resent you and everyone feels guilty!

If you think you have fallen into any of these traps and you aren't able to work your way out following our program, then you may need a more detailed approach to pain management. You could consult a specialist, go to a pain clinic or try reading a self-help book that focuses exclusively on pain management.

Coping Statements for Managing Pain

Preparing for pain
- ❖ What is my personal plan for dealing with pain?
- ❖ Just think through my plan.
- ❖ I have a number of techniques for managing pain.
- ❖ Don't worry about pain; worrying doesn't stop it.

Coping with pain
- ❖ I can handle it.
- ❖ Relax myself, breathe deeply and use a technique.
- ❖ Don't think about the pain, just think about what to do.
- ❖ Relax, I'm in control. Now, which technique will I use?

Coping with peaks of pain
- ❖ When the pain increases, switch to a different technique.
- ❖ Don't try to eliminate all pain, just manage it.
- ❖ Hold it, now which technique will I try?

After an episode of managing pain
- ❖ Good for me, I did it.
- ❖ I knew I could handle it.
- ❖ Now I should remember which techniques work best for me.

Grief

Grief is the normal human reaction to losing someone who has been emotionally important to you. As we consider in the next chapter, it is not unusual to grieve for the loss of a spouse through separation and divorce or for the loss of a close friend through moving. It is not even unusual to grieve for the loss of a family pet. However, in this chapter we focus on the grief caused by the death of a person of emotional significance in your life.

Grief is the normal reaction to loss. It is usually painful and distressing and it may take several years to resolve completely, but in itself it is not a problem that needs professional treatment. However, like other crisis reactions, it can become a serious problem if you don't manage it effectively. The aim of this discussion is to help you understand and work through your normal grieving process so you can avoid the possible complications that can occur in grief.

The grief response

Dr. James Averill and Dr. Patricia Wisocki, both professors of psychology at the University of Massachusetts, have summarized a lot of research into grief and proposed that it develops through four stages, or *components* (which are summarized in the box below). Other researchers have proposed different numbers of stages, but all of the descriptions are similar and you will recognize them as examples of the Crisis Response and Recovery Cycle (CRRC) stages.

The Grief Response

1. Shock

2. Protest and yearning

3. Disorganization and despair

4. Detachment and reorganization

The common first reaction is shock, although this is less pronounced if the death has been expected for some time. This shock period is characterized by a dazed sense of unreality or numbing that may last from a few hours to a few days. **weeks**

The second common reaction involves protest and yearning, because the loss is recognized but not entirely accepted. You are protesting your loss and may attempt to "recover" the dead person, at least symbolically. This stage often lasts for several months and. **/or years** and is marked by agitation and arousal. You may spend a lot of time

You may spend a lot of time thinking about the dead person, but are focusing on good memories, which increases your sense of loss.

thinking about the dead person, but are focusing on good memories, which increases your sense of loss.

Usually the longest and most difficult stage in the grief process comes next: disorganization and despair. Although you may accept the fact of loss and stop attempts to "recover" the dead person, you are left with a bitter pining for him. During this period people may suffer from apathy, withdrawal, despondency, loss of sexual interest, despair, hostility, shame and guilt as well as other problems.

Detachment and reorganization characterize the fourth and final stage. The distressing symptoms and problems of the previous stage fade as the bereaved person resolves new ways of thinking about herself and the world, and develops new relationships, new roles and a new sense of purpose. A person may take up to several years to readjust, even in cases of quite normal grief.

One of Australia's leading experts in the field of grief and bereavement is Beverley Raphael, professor of psychiatry at the University of Queensland. Based on her extensive research, her description of grief is similar to that above. She emphasizes the physical distress experienced by bereaved people, including difficulty breathing, palpitations, weakness and stomach problems. She points out that the anger in the protest stage may be felt toward the dead person for "abandoning" the bereaved person, and this in turn may make the bereaved person feel guilty. This anger is often displaced onto others, especially if the bereaved can see them as contributing to the death in some way.

The anxiety many bereaved people feel, Professor Raphael explains, results from feeling helpless about living without the dead person. A bereaved person may be preoccupied with images of the dead person, which may intrude into his consciousness. In response, some people try to avoid reminders of the dead person, which might be part of a general attempt to deny feelings. The guilt felt at this stage may be associated with regrets about past events in the relationship. If the bereaved person was involved with the dead person in the incident that caused death, he may also feel guilty for having survived.

When grief goes wrong

The points we want to emphasize are that grief is painful, long-lasting and variable but completely normal. Our advice for coping with the CRRC (see chapter 1) should help you work through your normal grief, and later in this chapter we offer a few specific suggestions for coping with grief. We begin by repeating our general advice: Accept and work through your normal feelings in response to this life crisis. Professor

> *The points we want to emphasize are that grief is painful, long-lasting and variable but completely normal.*

Raphael has described the complications that can occur if the crisis of grief is not worked through satisfactorily. These include

- Inhibited grief, resulting from over-control and bottled-up feelings, a state often misinterpreted by others as "coping well"

- Distorted grief, involving intense anger, especially after death in accidents or disasters

- Extreme preoccupation with guilt, involving repeated self-blaming

- Chronic grief, the most common complication, involving intense grief that goes on for months or years after the death

- Extreme and prolonged depression, when life does not seem worth continuing

- Post-traumatic stress disorders, which may occur with and complicate grief (see page 110)

If you are already grieving and you think you are at risk of one of these complications and our program does not help you to avoid or escape it, then it is time for you to seek professional help. Grief is normal and usually does not require professional counseling, but the complications of grief may be resolved with professional therapy. Meanwhile, here are suggestions to help you cope.

Suggestions for managing grief

If possible, visit the dying person before her death. Use the communication skills in chapter 9 to accept and understand her feelings, while being open about your own. Our rule of thumb is that dying people should be told honestly about their imminent death, so that they have the chance to work toward a personally appropriate death as we discuss in the first part of this chapter. During such a visit you may want to clear up any unfinished business—emotional and relational, not financial—but don't dump your unresolved personal problems on someone else.

If you have the opportunity and the dying person is close to you, be with him at the end. It gives you the chance to say goodbye and gives him the chance to say goodbye to you, too. You will know you were able to give him support right to the end. You may also be able to exchange support with other family and friends. You can't really apply this suggestion to yourself but you may help others if you can make sure the news of the death is conveyed carefully and supportively to them, preferably by someone who was present at the death.

In most cases, the use of heavy tranquilizers is inappropriate, for reasons we describe in chapter 7. Stopping your normal reactions by anesthetizing them only postpones them, sometimes making them worse. Rarely, a bereaved person's distress may be so agitated that temporary assistance with drugs is necessary, but that should be done only when it is genuinely in that person's interests and not to help others avoid the distress of the situation. This advice applies to the use of alcohol and other social drugs as much as to prescribed ones.

Most bereaved people benefit if they view the body, something that is generally offered by funeral homes. It is again a chance to say goodbye, especially for people who were not present at the death. Researchers have found that people generally manage their grief better after this chance than if they did not have it. While no one should be pressured to view the body, they should be encouraged to. If the body has been damaged in some way, it is still usually better to view it. Without that chance, bereaved people may upset themselves even more by imagining how badly it was damaged and how much the dying person may have suffered.

A funeral or similar event is usually the central event during the acute grief stage and it can help you to begin working through your grief.

If possible, attend the funeral or any similar formal ceremony. It again presents a chance to say goodbye, to give and receive support, and to begin the process of accepting your loss. A funeral or similar event is usually the central event during the acute grief stage and it can help you to begin working through your grief.

From here on, our general program for working through the CRRC is applicable. The support of others—family, friends or a community or self-help group—is important to most bereaved people (see the Resources section on page 215). Many find it helpful to share their feelings and have them understood and accepted by others. Make those opportunities for yourself. As a part of recovering from your loss, you may also need to do some practical problem-solving. The death of a spouse or parent may have an economic impact on you, or may require rearrangement of your lifestyle. Sometimes realizing that you have choices for rebuilding your life can be threatening in itself. Our suggestions in chapters 8, 9 and 10 should help.

Coping with the death of a child

Experts generally agree that the death of a child is one of the most tragic events that can happen to anyone. With the possible exception of the death of your spouse, it will cause you the greatest amount of anguish. Dr. Ronald Knapp, a sociologist at Clemson University in South Carolina, has made a study of families who lost children ranging in age from one to twenty-eight. He suggests that the death of a child is usually more traumatic because we don't expect children to die. Also, because a child's death is less common, people are even less prepared for coping with it.

While he found the normal diversity in the way people reacted to the deaths of their children, he did find six reactions common to most.

First was the desire of the parents never to forget their dead child. Mothers especially were frightened that their memories of the child would gradually fade.

Second was the need that developed in all the parents studied to talk about their loss, to share their feelings and have other people understand their reactions. Many bereaved parents did not discuss their loss when it would have been most helpful, sometimes because they did not want to upset others, sometimes because others did not want to share those discussions.

Open and constructive sharing of your feelings is essential for coping with this particular crisis.

Dr. Knapp concluded, as we have said, that open and constructive sharing of your feelings is essential for coping with this particular crisis.

Third was a reaction that tended to occur after the death of older children, in which the parents would contemplate their own deaths as a way of legitimizing the loss. Many of these parents were thinking, "Why my child? Why not me?" They often felt they could not justify continuing to live after the death of their child. These feelings of desolation and wanting to escape were usually strongest for the first two weeks to three months and were often followed by a nonchalant attitude toward death. Dr. Knapp believes that living with no fear of death may be a permanent characteristic of parents whose children died. Most did not actively seek their own deaths because they realized this would add to the suffering of other family members, and they recognized their continuing responsibilities to a spouse or other children. But some, especially mothers, remained apathetic toward and withdrawn from much of life.

Fourth, many parents tried to find some cause or plausible reason for their loss. It was an unusual family that could accept their child's death as just "fate," regardless of how the child had actually died. As in the stage of philosophical reflection in the CRRC, the victim is trying to make sense of his experience, to find reassurance that it was not all in vain. Dr. Knapp found that seven out of ten of the parents in his study eventually turned to religion for answers and comfort. For some, this was a continuance of previously held beliefs; for others, it was a personal religious revival or conversion.

The fifth reaction common to most parents was a noticeable change in values. Many parents questioned traditional values and goals for personal success and replaced them with more intangible values. Family goals tended to become more important than individual and career goals, and there was less concern with material objects and appearances. Many families developed a sense of vulnerability and came to see life and time as more precious. Parents often became more tolerant of others, and more sensitive to and understanding of others' problems.

Many families developed a sense of vulnerability and came to see life and time as more precious.

Finally, Dr. Knapp observed that most of the families were left with "shadow grief," a grief that did not dominate the parents' existences as it had right after the death, but that was never completely forgotten or resolved. It tended to show up in an emotional dullness, an inability to respond as fully as before and a moderate inhibition of normal activity. It could be brought to the surface by inner or outer reminders that produced sadness and mild anxiety, sometimes crying.

If your life crisis has been the death of your child, we hope the above discussion helps you to apply the program in this book to work through your grief. Dr. Knapp makes the point we have emphasized, that each individual's reaction to a crisis will be unique but not necessarily abnormal. With persistent effort on your part, including finding support from others, you should achieve the resolution of most of your grief.

Grieving for the unborn

Several situations have the potential to be grief crises but have not been recognized as such, at least until recently. About one in six pregnancies end prematurely, in miscarriage, tubal pregnancy or stillbirth. Many professional caregivers and family members have made the well-intended mistake of encouraging the woman (or the couple) to dismiss the event as a temporary setback, which results in blocking a natural and normal grief response. This can cause long-term problems, just as any unresolved crisis response can. (Women who give up babies for adoption experience a similar situation, and similar suggestions apply.)

Many pregnancies are also voluntarily terminated, for a range of medical, social and psychological reasons. Worldwide, abortion is the most widely used of all contraceptive measures. We do not intend to discuss the arguments about abortion because they are outside our professional field, although any doubts about the morality of her actions may add to any distress a woman experiences after an abortion. Many women see a voluntary termination as an acceptable contraceptive procedure. It has the normal stress associated with any surgical treatment but is not a crisis as such. For some, this is not so. We emphasize that we are not telling you how you should feel about an abortion. We do want you to understand that the normal range of reactions varies from comfortable acceptance to full-blown grief. So for you to have a reaction anywhere within that range makes you normal.

It has generally been assumed that the timing of the loss is important in these cases, that the longer the pregnancy has continued, the harder the loss is to cope with. Dr. Jack Stack, a psychiatrist with the Family Health Research Education and Service Institute in Michigan, has concluded that this is wrong, in light of his own research. He found that other factors about the pregnancy were more important, such as whether the pregnancy was wanted or planned, whether there had been previous miscarriages and how long it had taken to conceive. To understand the impact of the loss in these cases, one must ask what it meant to each of the partners.

Most felt the emotional impact immediately, although in a few cases it took a while to develop. In a study of women who had suffered miscarriages from two to twenty-one weeks after conception, nearly all the women reported sadness, and about 30 percent felt frustrated, disappointed or angry with themselves. Other researchers have also found that self-blame is a large part of the grief response in these cases, because often the woman's doctor cannot offer an explanation for what happened. Even women who are given explanations that emphasize that the miscarriage was an uncontrollable event may still experience guilt.

Several other factors about loss during pregnancy or at birth can complicate the grief reaction. First, early in pregnancy the woman may have told few people that she was pregnant, so she may be reluctant to discuss the loss and her feelings with many people later. Second, many women begin to fantasize about the coming baby, as do some men. After the loss, they mourn a fantasy, a child they never really knew. Some well-intended but misguided hospital staff will not allow the parents to view the body of a stillborn child, although this practice is now changing. Although men do not experience a pregnancy on the minute-by-minute basis a woman does, many find the loss just as difficult, especially when much of the available support may be directed toward the woman, making him feel that his loss does not or should not count.

> *After the loss, they mourn a fantasy, a child they never really knew.*

The relationship may be at risk if the partners react differently to the loss (which is not unusual in itself) and end up in conflict over their differences. For example, she may see his encouragement to renew activities as uncaring, while he may see her need to review the loss as obsessive, dragging him back into a hurt he wants to leave behind. Each feels misunderstood and unaccepted by the other, so they withdraw from each other just when mutual support would be most helpful. The antidotes for this are the communication skills we discuss in chapter 9.

> *She may see his encouragement to renew activities as uncaring, while he may see her need to review the loss as obsessive.*

Finally, the unresolved anxiety from your loss on this occasion can understandably resurface during subsequent pregnancies. Women who became pregnant again within four months of a miscarriage reported feeling vulnerable and unable to relax, especially as they approached the time at which they had previously miscarried.

You will recognize these reactions as examples of a natural grief response and, more generally, of the CRRC. The general program and the earlier suggestions in this chapter should be helpful to you. We emphasize the helpfulness of sharing your feelings—with each other, family, friends or self-help groups. Appropriate rituals can also help legitimize your grief: For example, naming your lost child, holding a memorial service or focusing on symbols, such as a set of footprints or a hospital bracelet. Throughout, don't allow well-intentioned but ill-informed people rob you of your rightful opportunity to grieve for your loss.

Coping with loss from suicide

Several factors about losing someone to suicide can make your grieving more difficult. First, suicides are sudden and unexpected deaths, even in cases when there may have been previous suicide attempts. It is not unusual for someone who has decided to commit suicide to experience a lift in mood because she has figured a way out of her unhappiness. When this lift in mood is understandably seen by others as evidence of improvement, the subsequent suicide comes as even more of a shock.

> *It is not unusual for you to imagine how he might have suffered, and therefore increase your own pain.*

Some people commit suicide in painful ways. It is not unusual for you to imagine how he might have suffered, and therefore increase your own pain. Some people also imagine the mental suffering that led up to the suicide.

Most suicides result from a mix of two motivations: to escape from a painful life that the person does not see as ever improving and to make an impact on those left behind, whether to free them from a burden or make them feel guilty. Sometimes these motives are made clear in a suicide message, sometimes they can be inferred from things said or done before the suicide. In any case, it is understandable that these aspects of suicide add to the grief of the survivors.

Anger is a normal component of the CRRC in general, and of grief in particular, and it occurs after suicides. It may be intensified because the dead person has not only died and left you, but she *chose* to die and most likely for reasons that are hard to understand or unacceptable to you. Then you are likely to feel guilty about feeling angry at someone who has died, presumably after considerable suffering.

Guilt is certainly a normal reaction. After a suicide, grief is often increased by the belief that you may have contributed to the dead person's emotional slide into suicide, or at least that you could have done something to prevent it. Some survivors will haunt themselves with memories of last conversations or times together, searching for some action they might have taken to tip the scales one way or the other. Parents of children who commit suicide are especially prone to self-blame, to search for evidence of their "mistakes."

> *Parents of children who commit suicide are especially prone to self-blame, to search for evidence of their "mistakes."*

When we counsel people in this situation, we make several points. First, to reach the level of depression and sense of hopelessness that lead to suicide, a person has usually been having problems for some time, often years. Other than in rare and exceptional circumstances, people do not suddenly decide to commit suicide because of a single event. A final conflict may have contributed to a long-term process leading to suicide, but it would not have been the sole or even a major cause. Some final action may have postponed the suicide but probably would not have prevented it.

So we encourage you to be realistic and fair when you judge yourself. You may have to accept that, like the rest of us, you have made some mistakes in your relationships, perhaps a few you will always regret. That makes you normal, like the rest of us. But also accept that you do not control anyone else's life, including your

Some final action may have postponed the suicide but probably would not have prevented it.

children's—you are only one of many influences in other people's lives. You cannot take responsibility for things you do not control, and trying to take responsibility for someone else's life and actions, however well intended, actually belittles and weakens that person. So try to be a good influence in others' lives, most of the time. Accept that you will sometimes fail and make mistakes, and that you may regret some of those, but that you can learn to live with them, as you can learn to live with your loss.

4

Coping with Marital and Family Crises

In this chapter we are guided by our definition of a crisis as an event that causes you to experience unusually strong emotional reactions, so strong that they interfere with your ability to function. Many problems that can occur in marital and family relationships may cause strong emotions, but not unusually strong. They can be serious problems that deserve constructive attention, but they are not crises as such and there are far too many of them for us to consider in a single book, let alone a chapter. If you are having serious relationship problems not dealt with here, we recommend trying other self-help books for improving relationships or seeking the advice of a family counselor. In this book, we discuss major family conflict, including domestic violence and incest, discovering an affair, separation and divorce.

Family Conflict, Arguments and Fights

Again, let's get our terms straight, because in this area they are often misunderstood. *Conflict* means the clash of opposing wants, goals, solutions, values or interests. *Some* conflict is inevitable in every human organization, including a couple or a family, because people living (or working) together rarely agree on every issue. In any case, conflict isn't necessarily bad. Having to explain your point of view and being willing to listen to someone else's can give you a better understanding of an issue. Exchanging ideas, or better still cooperatively working on them, can produce smarter solutions, prevent ruts and encourage creativity. Sticking up for your point of view effectively can build your self-esteem. Conflict can be a positive force.

Of course, it can also be a negative force, destroying relationships, damaging self-esteem, perhaps leading to violence. What counts is not whether you have conflict, because you will, but how you handle it. We use the term *arguments* in this chapter to mean a heated discussion of a conflict, in contrast to a calmer, problem-solving approach. Some couples we talk to insist that they have "no conflict" and are offended when we suggest that's unlikely. What they are reporting, perhaps correctly, is that they have no arguments. We hope this is because they are able to resolve their conflicts amicably and constructively, but sometimes it happens because one partner dominates the other.

> *What counts is not whether you have conflict, because you will, but how you handle it.*

Arguments do involve strong feelings and, if they become personally abusive or turn into power struggles, they can damage your relationship. They probably occur at least occasionally in most relationships and usually are not a life crisis of the kind we are considering in this book. Recent research has found that couples who work through a period of conflict by learning how to handle it constructively wind up with a stronger and more mutually satisfactory relationship.

Fights are arguments that have escalated to the point where physical or emotional violence is likely; both kinds of violence pose risks to your ability to function and are therefore crises. There isn't a clear dividing line between arguments and fights as we have described them. The question would be how strong your emotional reactions are, during and after the event. If they are getting strong enough to interfere with your ability to function, at the time or after, then you are facing a critical situation and the following discussion is for you.

Family fights

You may be frequently fighting with your partner or with someone else in the family. Poor handling of the usual conflict that develops between parents and adolescents, as the adolescents work toward their natural independence, often leads to escalating fights. Chronic family fighting is different from the situation of a battered spouse or child, which we discuss later in this chapter. Fighting is a two-way interaction, with both of the people involved attacking each other with physical or emotional violence. Battering tends to be one-way, with one person damaging the other, and results from different causes.

The risks in chronic family fights are that they become ingrained in family life and tend to escalate, with increasing risk of physical or emotional harm. For a long time, people have preferred to believe that family violence was rare and would only occur in unusual or "sick" families. There is now abundant evidence that this is not so. Violence occurs in many families from all socioeconomic groups and ethnic backgrounds. While there is a genuine risk of being the victim of a violent crime committed by a stranger (see chapter 2), you are much more likely to be assaulted by a family member.

> *Violence occurs in many families from all socioeconomic groups and ethnic backgrounds.*

In 1994, the United States Department of Justice reported that approximately 16 percent of homicides were murders within the family and about 40 percent of those were committed by a spouse. The family home was the scene of most violent incidents. In 1995, the National Clearinghouse for the Defense of Battered Women reported that the United States has 1,500 battered women shelters—and 3,800 animal shelters.

> *The United States has 1,500 battered women shelters—and 3,800 animal shelters.*

Perhaps because our culture has tended to glorify "the family," we don't want to admit that there might be something wrong within it. We traditionally see the family as "private," where outsiders should not intrude. It was not so long ago that *men and women* viewed the wife and children as the husband's possessions, to be treated as he saw fit.

Underneath these attitudes is a traditional belief in punishment, especially corporal punishment, as an effective and acceptable way of dealing with undesirable behavior. We won't debate its acceptability, but there is clear evidence that it is not effective. Some people misinterpret this research finding as an attack on "discipline." It isn't. We are all in favor of reasonable and rational discipline, preferably self-discipline. Our point is that punishment is not the way to encourage discipline and there is the risk that well-intended if misguided discipline may turn into family violence. Behind all these factors there seems to be a rising problem with violence in the general community, probably a reflection of our society's acceptance of violence, particularly in the entertainment media and spectator sports.

A factor that seems to have contributed to increased family violence has been the shrinking of the family to the "nuclear family," two adults living with their children (or some variation of this). Larger, extended families tend to have less family violence because other adults share the load and give each other support. A nuclear family can act as an emotional pressure cooker, in which there is only one other adult (sometimes none) to react with and seek support from. Modern families also tend to move more than families in the past did. They often become geographically isolated from relatives and may not develop alternative support within their neighborhoods. As a result of all these factors, when family violence does occur, the family members are likely to see themselves as unusual and abnormal, and they are often too ashamed to seek support.

> *Larger, extended families tend to have less family violence because other adults share the load and give each other support.*

Another factor often associated with family violence is alcohol abuse, or some other form of drug dependence. Alcohol or another drug doesn't directly cause the violence, but it reduces a person's self-control. The stress that often triggers family fights can also trigger increased drinking or drug use, just when you need more self-control, not less. While we repeat the observation that family violence occurs in all sections of society, it is more likely in working class and lower income families. This is because these are exactly the families more vulnerable to social stressors such as poverty, unemployment, financial insecurity, housing problems and so on.

> *The stress that often triggers family fights can also trigger increased drinking or drug use, just when you need more self-control, not less.*

Finally, there is the sad fact that the more violence a child experiences while growing up, the more likely the child will become a violent adult. At the time they are the recipients of family violence, many people vow that they will never be like their parents when they grow up, and they sincerely mean it. However, years later, when confronted with stress, the only example they have of how to react is one of lashing out violently and they find themselves repeating the pattern. Some also believe that loving relationships are violent ones, because of their past experiences. It is important to note that this is a trend and not an iron-clad guarantee. Many, but not all, of the people who become involved in family violence have previously been victims of family violence themselves. Some, but by no means all, of the victims of family violence will later act violently in their own families. But some do not. Having grown up in a violent family should not make you feel stuck with repeating the pattern, and it is certainly not an excuse for acting violently. You can understand why a behavior occurs without having to accept it.

> *Close observation of violent family fights shows some consistent patterns.*

Close observation of violent family fights shows some consistent patterns. A fight may begin with a relatively minor problem or conflict. At first both people are trying to solve the problem and resolve the conflict, but they do it in ways that further upset or frustrate each other and gradually the fight becomes a struggle for control. Each sees himself as the innocent victim of the other's provocation. Fights may also be triggered by breaches of the family "rules," the expectations that have developed over how each family member should behave. If the rule is a spoken one, breaking it usually provokes an immediate, angry reaction. If the rule is an unspoken one, the reaction is usually delayed and harder for both people to understand.

Strangely enough, a common trigger for fighting in couples is fear of losing the relationship.

Strangely enough, a common trigger for fighting in couples is fear of losing the relationship. One partner, who believes he is unloved or unlovable—partly in reaction to the other partner's behavior and partly as a result of his own early experiences—will react strongly to real or imagined threats of losing the relationship. Since the root of his fear lies in his own self-image, no response from his partner will lessen his fears and so the fight escalates. In the end, he may bring about exactly the outcome he feared: His partner may leave him.

Popular myths about fighting can escalate situations. Although they may not say so in these words, many people suffering from family fights effectively believe ideas such as "If I hit her, she will realize how much I love her," or "If I throw something at him, he will understand how hurt I feel," or "If I leave (or threaten to leave), it will scare her and make her change." In fact, the actions they take based on these myths aggravate the situation, being seen by the other person as an attack on his security or control. A similar myth can build up around a couple's sexual relationship, when sex is used to make up after a fight and they wind up with a pattern of intimacy that can only occur after a fight.

In most family fights there appears to be a "victim" and a "villain" (depending on whose point of view you take), when in fact you are looking at a shared problem. Both may truly love each other and want the relationship to be successful, but they have developed a pattern of interacting with each other that creates and escalates fights. If you look carefully at the descriptions above, you will identify certain recurring elements:

- Unrealistic self-talk about yourself and the other person's feelings and intentions toward you

- Sometimes a personal problem dealing with anger

- A lack of effective communication resulting in a lack of mutual understanding

- A lack of negotiation and problem-solving skills, resulting in a lack of mutually acceptable resolutions or any resolution at all

We have compiled step-by-step instructions for making your self-talk more realistic (chapter 8), managing your anger (chapter 10) and communicating and negotiating (chapter 7). We do encourage people to try self-help because solving your problems for yourself is not only cheaper than seeking professional help, it does great things for your self-esteem. But we add a note of caution. People in a relationship marked by lots of conflict often cannot cooperate enough to follow a self-help program. Sometimes the self-help program becomes something else to fight about. If the conflict has been damaging, one of them may no longer feel the commitment necessary to work on a self-help program.

People are often reluctant to admit they are having a problem with family violence, for all the reasons discussed earlier. Chronic fighting in a couple can result from a relationship that is obviously troubled but also very dependent, and the couple close ranks and deny their problem to outsiders. If self-help gets you tackling your problem of family violence instead of denying it, that's an important step forward. But if you can't get it started, or it looks like it's not working, we strongly encourage you to get outside help. We have focused on the risk of physical damage resulting from family violence, because that has been most studied, but we have also referred to the risk of emotional damage, because in some ways that may be worse, at least in its long-term effects. Even if no one is seriously physically hurt by your family fights, you will all probably carry emotional scars. You may even be setting up your children to become the next generation of violent families, and we're sure that's not what you want to do. So bite the bullet and talk to someone.

Battered spouses

As we pointed out earlier, *battering* is different from fighting. Battering involves deliberate, severe and repeated physical injury, usually of a woman or child. Although researchers now agree that there are more instances of violence by women toward men than used to be thought, it usually happens as a part of a fight rather than as a part of battering. Battering is usually an adult male inflicting physical injury on a woman, or an adult inflicting physical injury on a child, without the victim fighting back, except in some attempt at self-defense. The risk of serious physical injury is real and of major concern. However, we again add our concern about the psychological damage that may be left, long after physical wounds have healed.

One careful study of a hundred battered women found that many of the attacks they had suffered were sudden, uncontrolled outbursts of rage, but some were premeditated, with the man trying to inflict injuries that left no visible marks, by hitting the woman above the hairline or on the lower back. All the women had bruises, many had lacerations and quite a few had suffered fractures. Many of their children were described as "disturbed," with a variety of problems including temper tantrums, bedwetting, vandalism, stealing and "vicious fighting." In the light of findings like these, the most common reaction is to ask why these women stay in the battering situations and why, after they have left, so many return. This reaction is understandable but reflects a lack of understanding of the problem.

> *Researchers have found that, over time, a battered woman begins to accept her partner's thinking.*

Many battering men seem to love their partners sincerely. After a battering incident they may show great remorse and act in loving ways. Some will explain their behavior as being a result of their love; some say the woman "needed it"; and some come from subcultures in which beating is seen as a demonstration of love. Researchers have found that, over time, a battered woman begins to accept her partner's thinking. This is even more true when, as is often the case for adults who stay in abusive relationships, they were previously abused as children. They have learned to associate loving relationships with physical abuse.

These relationships have common patterns. Sometimes the man was attracted to the woman because of her submissiveness, but later he finds her inability to take responsible initiative increasingly frustrating. She responds to his anger by being more submissive and he in turn becomes angrier. Alternatively, a man with low self-esteem may be attracted to a woman because she seems capable and strong. However, he then finds her competence is a threat to him and reacts angrily. She responds by trying to be more competent, which further angers him. In both patterns, her attempt to do "the right thing," the behavior that previously worked in the relationship, now provokes further abuse. In the absence of real understanding of each other's feelings and wants, they become locked into a vicious cycle.

In both patterns, her attempt to do "the right thing," the behavior that previously worked in the relationship, now provokes further abuse.

The simple suggestion that the woman should just leave is unrealistic. Most battered women have no career nor any prospect of one and would face considerable financial hardship. They often also have major responsibility for one or more children, and fear for the children's safety if they were left with the man. They may have good reason to fear a violent reaction from the man if they do leave. They usually feel isolated and trapped in the situation.

Psychologists working in this field have found that the typical battered woman will make between three and five attempts to leave home before she is capable of actually sticking to her decision. Yet it is important that she does take decisive action, for her own sake, her children's sake and even for the man's sake. Battering men are usually resistant to accepting their problem, at least at first, and some never accept it. Often the only real leverage she has to make him face up to his problem is to leave and to stay away, at least until he has constructively tackled the problem.

If being battered is your life crisis, we encourage you to rethink the situation, in particular to question your partner's explanation for his actions. You almost certainly do contribute to the problems in your relationship, *but that does not excuse his violence*. We understand that you may find it hard to believe that you can get by without this relationship, but the truth is you can. In fact, you would almost certainly be better off without the relationship in its present state. If he will not accept that his violence is a problem he needs to tackle, then you may be giving

> *Your situation is not unique and you can do something about it, even if it's difficult to begin.*

your relationship its best chance if you leave it, at least until he does something about his problem. If you need support, which you probably will, consult a psychologist or counselor or go to a women's group or shelter. Every one of the hundred women in the study we mentioned thought her situation was unique, and way beyond solving. Your situation is not unique and you can do something about it, even if it's difficult to begin.

Violent men, and their partners, can take heart from a recent Australian study of twenty-six men undergoing a three-month group therapy program. These men reported being able to accept their problems and seek help because of the support of meeting other men in a similar situation. Several months after the program ended, the men said they were able to handle their emotions and communicate better, and they were spending more time with their families. All forms of violence had decreased or stopped. There is light at the end of the tunnel, if you will start walking down it.

Battered children

The physical abuse of children by their parents or other caretakers is another aspect of family violence that we as a society prefer to ignore or assume is a rare phenomenon in "sick" families. Once again, research has confronted us with an uglier truth: Physical abuse of children is a widespread problem, occurring in all areas of society. One expert recently estimated that, at any one time, one million children are being abused or neglected in the United States. The U.S. Department of Health and Human Services estimates that children under three years old account for 75 percent of child abuse fatalities.

We are not referring simply to strict punishment. We have already made clear our opinion, based on a large body of research, that corporal punishment is not an effective way of either improving behavior or building discipline. Plenty of people in our society still believe in physical punishment and will use it *within humane limits*, even if it is in vain. Child abuse refers to inflicting physical injury on a child, resulting in observable damage, ranging from bruises to life-threatening injuries. Again we add our concern for the psychological damage that can also be inflicted by emotional abuse.

Just as our society glorifies "the family," it tends to glorify parenthood—many people can't understand how any *adult*, let alone many of them, could deliberately injure a child. These popular misunderstandings about the frequency and causes of child abuse often make abusive parents more secretive about and willing to deny their problem. Abusive families often close ranks and try to resist outside attempts to help.

> *Abusive families often close ranks and try to resist outside attempts to help.*

There is a lot of evidence that abusive parents were often abused as children. Although they may have vowed they would not be like their parents, when they finally have to cope with the normal stresses of raising children, the old example of their own parents emerges. *Again we emphasize that this does not have to be the case and it is certainly not an excuse for abusing your own children.*

Many abusive parents have low self-esteem and see themselves as failures in general, not only as parents. Many suffer periods of depression. Perhaps as a result of poor relationships with their own parents, they often have trouble understanding their children's feelings, wants and behavior. Some of these parents tend to see adultlike motives underlying what was really typically childlike behavior. They often don't understand what is normal behavior for children at different ages.

Abusive parents are usually isolated from family and friends. The only other adult with whom they have much contact is often their spouse and many have serious marital problems that may not be obvious. Sometimes a battering mother is herself a battered wife, and she is using her child as a scapegoat. Some researchers have found that many abusive mothers experienced a premature or difficult birth, which may have resulted in their being separated from their babies. The babies themselves may have truly been more difficult or demanding, and all of this can weaken the woman's belief in her competence as a mother.

The picture of an abusive parent that emerges from research is very different from the ogre of popular imagination. They are mostly sad, isolated, lonely and fearful people, who were often themselves victims of abuse or neglect. They often lack family and social support but, because of their isolation and low self-esteem, have trouble asking for the help they need. Most abusive parents are people who love their children very much but who are unable to control themselves in stressful situations.

> *Most abusive parents are people who love their children very much but who are unable to control themselves in stressful situations.*

If child abuse is your life crisis, we hope this information helps you understand that there is an explanation for why you are hurting your children and there is something you can do to stop it. We understand that your fear of other people's reactions to your behavior can make it hard to seek help, but you owe it to yourself and your children. You may be pleasantly surprised at the supportive and understanding response you will receive and you will see that the emphasis today is on keeping troubled families together, if possible, not on taking children away from their parents.

In a similar vein, if you are not an abusive parent but you know it is happening, perhaps because it involves your partner, you have an overriding responsibility to the children affected. Adults do have some choice and can take responsibility for themselves; children do not and cannot. We encourage you to make a supportive approach to the abusive adult, to try to get her to seek help. If she won't do that, you must report the situation to a responsible authority. However unpleasant, you are really doing the best for everyone involved.

Sexual abuse and incest

As recently as 1975, a psychiatric textbook claimed that child sexual abuse occurred in one family in a million. Just as we don't want to accept the possibility that violence occurs in many families, we also don't want to accept the extent of child sexual abuse and the fact that most of it occurs within the family. Several research studies found 25 to 35 percent of American women and 10 to 16 percent of American men had experienced some sexual abuse as children, ranging from sexual fondling to intercourse. Some experts believe even these figures underestimate the problem, because children are often reluctant to report being sexually abused, even later as adults.

Most child sexual abuse victims are between nine and twelve years old, although some are much younger. The abuser is almost always a man, usually known to the child and often a family member.

Child sexual abuse occurs in all socioeconomic and ethnic groups. Once again there is the sad tendency for abusive adults to have been sexually abused themselves as children, although again there are exceptions.

There has been some controversy about whether children make up stories about being sexually abused to get back at an adult, or to gain attention. From our reading of the research, we have concluded that most reports by children of sexual abuse are true. It is unlikely that young children could give a detailed account of sexual assault without having experienced it. Our rule of thumb is to assume that the child is more likely to be telling the truth than lying, although each case should be considered thoughtfully because a false accusation can also be traumatic for the adult. There have been a few cases when a separated or feuding parent has coached a child to make complaints about the other parent. There is also the risk that a well-intentioned but poorly trained doctor, counselor or police officer may use leading questions that produce false answers. Because the reaction of adults in a child victim's life is one of the major factors influencing his recovery, it is always best if he is interviewed by someone with appropriate training.

Controversy also exists over whether children who have been sexually abused are necessarily harmed in the long term. For example, Dr. Chris Bagley, professor of social welfare at the University of Calgary in Canada, estimated that 50 percent of women who were sexually abused as children did not suffer long-term effects. That means that 50 percent were adversely affected. Adults who were sexually abused as children tend to have lower self-esteem and often suffer anxiety, depression and guilt. Many of the women who were abused as children are later the victims of rape or attempted rape. It seems that they don't know how to protect themselves. They were also likely to have children who were in turn sexually abused.

Many of the men who were abused wind up confused about their sexual identity, deeply ashamed, unwilling to report the experience and inclined to react aggressively. Some child sexual abuse victims later show many of the signs of the post-traumatic stress disorder usually seen in combat veterans, including flashback memories, recurring dreams, alienation and a sense of numbness.

Adults who are caught sexually abusing children and some organizations for pedophiliacs (adults sexually attracted to children) have argued that their child sexual partners are willing participants and are not harmed by the experience. Some of them will point out other civilizations in which adult-child sexual relations are accepted. This is all a smokescreen to justify behavior that is unacceptable. While it is true that some children are willing participants, that reflects their immaturity and ignorance rather than truly informed consent. Many of these children are seeking affection and acceptance, not sexual relations. In any case we believe the responsibility falls squarely on the adult, as the grown-up and more mature person in the situation, to recognize the inappropriateness and riskiness of accepting a child's sexual overtures or availability. It is absolutely clear that many children who are sexually abused do suffer long-term adverse effects, even if some escape. We do not think it is acceptable for an adult to gamble with a child's future well-being for the sake of personal gratification.

Researchers have found the following factors influence the severity of the child's reaction to being sexually abused and therefore his risk of long-term effects.

- **Age:** Younger children seem more vulnerable to long-term effects.

- **Emotional maturity:** Children who have had other emotional problems are more vulnerable.

- **Previous sexual experience:** Children with no previous sexual experience are more vulnerable.

- **Amount of violence:** The more violence, the greater the risk of long-term effects.

- **Repetition:** Being sexually abused many times, or by more than one adult, increases the risk of damage.

- **Familiarity:** The risk of damage increases the better the child knows the abuser, being worst with a close relative.

- **Age of the abuser:** Victims are most affected if the abuser is between twenty-six and fifty years old.

- **Reactions of others:** Negative reactions from parents, teachers, friends or police can increase the trauma.

- **Professional help:** Victims who receive appropriate counseling or therapy are more likely to recover completely than those who do not.

Experts agree that two signs strongly suggest sexual abuse has happened, whenever they occur together. The first is a preoccupation with sex, which may be revealed by frequent masturbation, perhaps in public, or an unusually high interest in sexual organs, sex play and nudity. The second is to be suffering from a number of physical problems, such as rashes, vomiting and headaches, without any apparent medical explanation. If you are not sure whether a child is being sexually abused, the occurrence of both of those signs would strongly suggest she is.

From this discussion you will see that you can do several things if your life crisis is the fact that your child has been sexually abused. It is most important that your reactions to the child are understanding and supportive, not angry, blaming or critical. Many parents unintentionally add to their children's problems by reacting, understandably but unfortunately, in negative ways: "Why didn't you come and tell me?" "How could you have been so silly?" "Why did you let yourself get into that position?" The effect is to make the child feel even more guilty and self-blaming, which is not really what you want.

Most parents of sexually molested children will benefit from counseling, at least for themselves, so that they learn how to give their children necessary support and guidance. Discussion with your counselor will help you decide whether your child also needs counseling. You should try to strike a balance between avoiding any unnecessary fuss about what has happened and avoiding the risk of denying what has happened and its potential for harm. That can be a difficult balancing act, so consider talking to a qualified clinical psychologist or some other appropriate counselor. There are sexual assault centers and women's shelters in most cities and several hotlines for reporting and discussing child abuse (see the Resource section on page 215).

Adults who have sexually abused a child are likely to do so again, unless they receive effective treatment. We encourage you to report the situation to the police or a sexual assault center. We realize this can be difficult, especially if the adult involved is a close relative or friend, but we hope you will agree that you have a responsibility to try to protect his present and future victims. The situation is most difficult if your spouse has been sexually abusing your child. Incest represents a basic breach of trust in family relationships, so its discovery can cause strong emotional reactions.

You may want to escape from your spouse, or you may be scared of losing him, or you may feel just plain confused. You will almost certainly benefit from counseling for yourself. At the least, this situation places all the more responsibility on you, as the other parent, to do the right thing by your child. The emphasis today is on helping families solve problems like these and stay together, if that's possible and desirable, but nothing will improve unless someone takes firm action. That someone should be you.

> *Nothing will improve unless someone takes firm action. That someone should be you.*

Adolescents like to present themselves as mini-adults, but as their parents know, they still have some childlike needs. Adolescence is also the life stage of sexual awakening, so a bad sexual experience at this time can have long-term effects, especially if it is the adolescent's first sexual experience. For these reasons it is important that adolescent sexual abuse victims also receive a lot of support, particularly from their parents and possibly from a counselor. Adolescent victims are sometimes reluctant to report being raped because they fear their parents' negative reactions or because the offender was one of their peer group. A positive, accepting and supportive approach gives your adolescent the best chance of opening up and being able to deal with her crisis.

Adolescent disasters

Some conflict between parents and their adolescent children is normal. In fact, we would worry about a family in which no conflict occurs because it may mean the adolescent's normal growth of independence has been squashed. Typically, the conflict starts when the child goes through puberty and starts to flex her independent wings. In a year or two, everyone has more or less adjusted to her new life stage, and family life rolls on. For a minority of families, that readjustment

> *Some conflict between parents and their adolescent children is normal.*

doesn't happen. The conflict between parents and adolescents steadily gets worse, until family life is tense and unhappy most of the time. This situation may become a family crisis when the adolescent announces that he is leaving home or, worse, just runs away without saying anything. There is a real risk that he may become a street kid and drift into a disastrous lifestyle.

Preferably you should not let things get this far. If the conflict between parents and adolescents in your family shows no signs of lessening, but seems to be getting worse, take constructive action. Try one of several self-help books for dealing with teenage conflict or see a qualified clinical psychologist or family counselor. If family relations have reached the point where you must accept that you cannot live together in a workable way, then even that becomes a problem you can solve constructively. If your adolescent cannot live with you, where can you all agree she should live? With grandparents, uncles, aunts, friends of the family? It's better to try to solve this problem in a mutually acceptable way than to come home and find she is long gone.

Other adolescent life crises include quitting school, pregnancy, and drug use. Each of these situations can prompt strong emotional reactions and, if handled badly, has the potential to cause long-term problems for both of you. Managing your own bad feelings (chapter 8), learning to communicate clearly (chapter 9) and recognizing that she is no longer a child will give you the best chance of working through this crisis together.

Discovering an affair

A crisis that occurs in many people's lives at some time is discovering that their partner is having another relationship, an "affair." Such victims feel angry because of the deception and breach of trust; they may feel anxious because they fear losing the relationship; they may suffer a severe loss of self-esteem and become depressed, seeing themselves as having lost their partner's love.

For her part, the partner having the affair also has strong emotions: often a strong attraction to both the outside partner and the spouse, guilt over the deception and hurt involved, and massive confusion about what to do. Some people wallow in this dilemma for months, sometimes moving backward and forward from one relationship to the other, to the considerable stress of all, especially any children. The problem for both spouses is that something needs to be done, but extreme emotional upset and confusion are not the best circumstances for any worthwhile problem-solving. All too often the situation is resolved in a peak of anger or hurt or confusion, resulting in a decision that is later regretted, perhaps by everybody.

All too often the situation is resolved in a peak of anger or hurt or confusion, resulting in a decision that is later regretted, perhaps by everybody.

So let us try to inject rational problem-solving into the situation, if this is your life crisis. As in other crises, we encourage you to accept the normality of your feelings, but to manage them (see chapter 8) and express them constructively (see chapter 9). Above all, we discourage you from making important decisions on the spur of the moment, while experiencing peaks of bad feelings. On the other hand, we also discourage you from doing nothing, hoping the problem will go away or resolve itself for you. Your primary relationship is too important a part of your life for you to surrender its decisions to other people.

Your primary relationship is too important a part of your life for you to surrender its decisions to other people.

If you are the spouse who has discovered the affair, we understand how bad you feel. We want you to interpret the situation realistically. We have never seen someone get involved in an affair unless there was *already* something wrong with his primary relationship. People stray outside the relationship because some important want is not being met at home. Discovering an affair is painful, but it also gives you important information: "There must have been something wrong with our relationship for my partner to get involved in an outside relationship." If you are both willing to see the situation as a solid warning and try to figure out what has gone wrong and do something constructive about it, you may eventually be able to lay your present crisis to rest as an ugly memory that did have some positive results.

If you are the spouse who has been having the affair, we sympathize with the confusion you are probably feeling. Many people in your situation end up hopelessly confused: "Do I belong in this relationship or that one?" Many then make the mistake of trying to compare the two relationships to help them make up their minds. Such comparisons are invalid and useless. They will only add to your confusion and give you a headache. We advise you to recognize that you are facing two distinct questions and you should tackle them one after the other.

First, ask yourself: "Do I think there is a reasonable chance that my marriage might work well for me? If I do, I owe it to myself to work on it." If your partner is willing, try to figure out what went wrong and see if you can fix it to the satisfaction of both of you. If you can, you have resolved your dilemma and rebuilt your relationship stronger than it was before the affair. If you can't, at least you can leave your primary relationship knowing that you gave it your best shot. Then you can ask yourself the second question, "Can I make a good long-term relationship with my new partner?" You can't really answer that question on the basis of the sort of meetings and activities that usually occur in affairs.

Notice the order: First decide whether your primary relationship can work for you. If the answer is "No," then decide whether your new relationship has any real long-term prospects. If you and your spouse decide to work on your relationship, we strongly advise you to put the other relationship on hold. If you want to give your primary relationship its best chance, it needs your undivided attention. You should say to your new companion that you are confused—she probably knows that already—and that you are going to resolve your confusion by first trying to save your marriage. To do that right, you will not be having any contact with her for about three months. Tell her you understand she will probably feel bad about this, as you do, but it's the best way to resolve your dilemma. If it turns out that your marriage can't be saved, then you will be free for a new relationship, with no doubts or strings attached. Let her know that you realize she may not be willing to wait three months, but you hope she can see this way is best for all involved.

And believe us, it is. You both need to accept that the affair is a symptom of a troubled relationship, not the cause of it. Like all distressed couples, you have three choices and you cannot avoid making one of them.

> *You both need to accept that the affair is a symptom of a troubled relationship, not the cause of it.*

1. You can agree to work on your relationship, see a qualified psychologist or marriage counselor or try self-help using a book that focuses exclusively on marital problems.

2. One or both of you may not believe the relationship will work and so you can call it quits, preferably calmly and constructively.

3. You can stew over your dilemma and do nothing constructive.

People making this third choice sometimes kid themselves that they are doing nothing, but it is a real choice with real consequences: maximum stress for everyone involved. We strongly discourage you from making choice number three; if you can't pick between the other two, that usually means you should try number one. Working on a distressed relationship is the best way to decide if you belong in it.

The question that often arises in the aftermath of an affair is one of trust. "How can I ever trust her again after she did this to me?" The answer is you can only find out by trying. Trust is not a right that people can simply expect or demand, and it is not usually present at the start of a relationship. Don't confuse trust with gullibility and wishful thinking. Trust is something you earn by behaving in a trustworthy way, and that takes time. The paradox about trust in relationships is that, if you want to build (or rebuild) it, you have to behave as if it is already there. You have to stick your neck out and behave in ways that make you vulnerable and that give your partner the chance to let you down (again). Only then can she act in ways that show you she did not let you down (again), even though the chance was there. Then you have the solid evidence on which you can base realistic trust. You need to say something to yourself along the lines of "I feel very bad about the way my partner let me down and I feel anxious that it might happen again, but I understand that I have to give her the chance to show she isn't going to let me down again. I do want to keep this relationship, if we can rebuild the trust in it, so I'll take that chance."

The paradox about trust in relationships is that, if you want to build (or rebuild) it, you have to behave as if it is already there.

In the end, you may have to decide or accept that your relationship is over. The grief reaction to losing a relationship through separation and divorce is similar to the reaction to loss caused by death of your partner. So the suggestions in chapter 3 should fit your crisis of losing a relationship. The only variation is to beware of the common mistake of misinterpreting a loss due to separation and divorce as being some personal devaluation, and thinking that your partner is leaving the relationship because there is something wrong with you. That kind of self-talk is only going to add to your distress and depression and it has no real basis. Who says your ex-partner is the world's judge of what is desirable and attractive in other people? If you find you are having many self-devaluing thoughts like those, try the ideas in chapter 8. Meanwhile, follow the steps in chapter 3 to begin rebuilding your life, at a realistic pace.

Who says your ex-partner is the world's judge of what is desirable and attractive in other people?

Most of the family crises considered in this chapter are different in important ways from the other life crises we have described in the book. You need to adapt the CRRC to fit your personal situation.

5

Coping with
Life-Stage Crises

Everyone's heard of the "midlife crisis," but most don't realize
that at any number of life stages a person can have problems,
perhaps even a crisis. Most of us get through each stage eventually,
even middle age. Other life stages include starting school,
moving from primary to secondary school, puberty, starting to
date, beginning sexual relations, starting work or college, leaving
home, getting married, having your first baby, changing jobs,
getting fired, menopause, divorce, your kids leaving home, and
retiring from work.

You may remember some of these life events, or even be
in the middle of one or two right now. You may remember or
even be having strong emotional reactions as a result. For the
most part you will probably agree that, even if they were difficult,
they were not *crises* as we define them in this book. On the other
hand, even life events we do not mention will trigger a crisis for
some people. For some men, the clear evidence that they are
going bald will provoke a crisis reaction, sometimes leading to
useless but expensive attempts to turn back the tide of their
genes and hormones.

We focus on a few life stages that have the greatest risk of
becoming crises for a number of people. We hope to not only help
those who suffer the life-stage crises we address but also provide a
more general framework you can adapt to your own situation, if it
is not one we consider here in detail. The basic formula of the

Crisis Response and Recovery Cycle (CRRC) will help you, if you choose steps to fit your needs from our general program in chapters 7 to 11. Then flesh these steps out with information about your particular crisis. Meanwhile, we will consider the midlife crisis, depression during menopause, having to move and losing your job.

Midlife Crisis

The midlife crisis is a pop psychology favorite. Like most of the ideas in that field, *midlife crisis* is usually loosely defined and associated with other problems that just *happen* to be occurring in middle age. For example, some middle-aged people suffer from burnout, the stress-induced exhaustion that tends to happen to overcommitted people who set unrealistic standards for themselves. Some young adults suffer burnout, too, as well as some older ones. It isn't necessarily a crisis of midlife. It doesn't really help a problem just to give it a new name, no matter how trendy that name may be. So we try to focus on what we have seen as the crisis characteristic of midlife, although this crisis by no means happens to everyone at this life stage.

Some young adults suffer burnout, too, as well as some older ones. It isn't necessarily a crisis of midlife.

What we have observed occurring in midlife rather than in younger or older adulthood is a crisis in life goals. This crisis seems to come in two forms.

Some people start out in adult life with goals they achieve by middle age, perhaps easily. They are often wealthy, with all the material signs of personal success. Yet they are unhappy, frequently depressed and restless. In a sense, they are saying, "I have spent my life working toward these goals and now that I have them, I should be feeling great, but I'm not. Is something wrong with me? Was it all pointless? A big mistake?" The strength of their feelings interferes with their present ability to function and they are at risk of making hasty decisions about career, property and relationships that could cause them later problems. They are suffering a genuine midlife crisis.

The other group that suffer crisis at middle age consists of people who also started out with a particular set of goals but who are coming to terms with the fact that they will probably never achieve them. The goals were, in fact, unrealistic, although that may not have been so obvious at the time. After all, our culture is filled with stories of people who rose to success from humble beginnings, the man or woman who started out broke and became a zillionaire. Most companies try to motivate their employees with the promise of apparently unlimited promotion. If you have the ability and put in the effort, they say, you too can climb to the top of the ladder.

The trouble with these modern fairy tales is that most organizations, and our society in general, are not shaped like a ladder but more like a pyramid. They get increasingly narrow the closer you get to the top. While the lower rungs may have had plenty of room for lots of people, the higher rungs have less and less room. Fewer people keep moving up, and eventually some people have to realize that they are probably not going to move up any further. For some, this brings on a crisis. "If all of my life has been about achieving these goals and now I have to accept that I'm probably not going to achieve them, what was it all about? Does this mean I have failed?" The latter part of their self-talk has an obvious potential for triggering depression. These people, too, are suffering a genuine midlife crisis.

Despite some differences, both of these midlife crises center around goals. The first group have achieved theirs, sometimes too soon and too easily. The second group have to give up on theirs, sometimes bitterly. What they both lack are current goals that appeal to them, motivate them and give some meaning to their lives. Midlife crisis is essentially a crisis of goallessness.

> *Midlife crisis is essentially a crisis of goallessness.*

Many people think only business people and large corporations set goals. Often, when we first suggest goal-setting to people, many of them think we are trying to sell them a motivational course, something irrelevant to them as ordinary people. In fact, it is impossible to be alive and not set *some* goals. If you roll yourself out of bed in the morning and think, "I'll go to the bathroom, make breakfast and try to catch the 8:40," or "I'll defrost a roast and put it in the oven for dinner tonight," you are setting goals. Making any concrete plans to achieve any clear outcome is goal-setting.

Many of us restrict our goal-setting to the more immediate, day-to-day side of life without much thought about how these daily goals may help us reach or block larger life goals. Many of us also tend to set goals in reaction to events and pressures on us, rather than as an initiative to take more charge of our lives. It's more often a case of "Oops, that's gone wrong," or "Oh boy, that needs to be done. So now what will I do about this?" rather than "What do I want to achieve next in this part of my life?"

We have called this the *jellyfish approach* to goal-setting and life. A jellyfish spends its life being carried around by currents and weather. If a fish swims into its tentacles, it will respond by catching and eating it, so it is active, but only in reaction to the fish's arrival. Although the jellyfish pumps itself along through the water, it does not actually hunt its prey. It just increases its chances of being lucky, like a human buying a lottery ticket.

You can take more charge of your life, build and sustain motivation and enjoy more personal success if you are willing to accept that you are already setting goals anyway, so you might as well do it skillfully.

Right now, if you are having a midlife crisis, focus on chapters 8 and 10 for ideas on managing your bad feelings, and chapter 9 for ideas on how not to let your crisis become everybody else's. Those steps are all-important and deserve your careful attention. However, you also need to do something about goallessness, the trigger of your midlife crisis. You have to set goals, either because you need to replace the goals you have already achieved with new ones, or because you need to replace some unrealistic and unattainable goals with goals you can achieve.

Setting life goals

Goal-setting is a practical skill that many of us could stand to brush up on. Statements such as "I would like to earn more money" or

"I wish my marriage were more fun" are not goals. We call them "wants" and you *do* need them to begin goal-setting, but they are not useful or usable goals. Useful and usable goals have five characteristics that make them work.

1. Make your goals realistic. They should be likely for you to achieve, given your abilities and life circumstances. Nothing builds and sustains motivation more than enjoying the success of achieving a goal, sending you off to work toward the next goal. Don't worry about setting your goals too low, because goal-setting is a never-ending process: As soon as you achieve this one, you replace it with the next one. If, for example, your goal is to improve your tennis skills so you can play on your club's B-team, when in fact you have the ability to play on the A-team, that's no problem. Once you achieve your first goal and join the B-team, you could then set yourself a new goal of more improvement so you can join the A-team. On the other hand, there is considerable risk in setting your goals too high. Nothing destroys motivation like failure. Humans don't really learn from mistakes; they usually just get discouraged. Make enough mistakes, or fail at enough unrealistic goals, and you will just stop trying. One of the common symptoms of the midlife crisis is a lack of motivation.

> *As soon as you achieve this one, you replace it with the next one.*

2. Set goals you can achieve reasonably soon. If you have ever taken part in a race, you know how you can save an extra burst of effort for when you get close to the finish, something called the "end spurt." In contrast, a distant goal you can't achieve for a while tends to be a poor motivator. If one of your wants is necessarily distant—for example, to earn a four-year degree—then you need to set sub-goals along the way, such as completing the first semester successfully. Aim for your sub-goals one at a time, get the benefit of the end spurt as you approach each, enjoy the success of achieving each and you will keep your motivation and effort consistently high. Then, presto! Before you know it, you are achieving your main goal, which may have seemed too distant otherwise.

3. Set goals that reflect your interests. As you would expect, you are more motivated to work on and will gain more enjoyment from activities you find interesting. This may seem obvious, but you would be surprised at how many people end up struggling with goals that do not reflect their interests because they were the wrong personal choice in the first place, or they have gradually lost their appeal. You may need to spend time clarifying your current interests. Start by asking yourself the following questions:

- Which of my present activities give me the most enjoyment or satisfaction? Which give me the least?

- If I could spend a day doing anything I liked, what would I do? (Try to come up with several answers.)

- Are there any activities I have never done that I think I might like to try?

4. Set goals that match your values, your sense of right and wrong. It's difficult to motivate yourself to do things you don't believe in and afterward you may feel guilty, or at best dissatisfied. On the other hand, goals you have no moral reservations about will get you going wholeheartedly. Again, to meet this guideline, spend a little time clarifying your values, especially if you haven't thought about them much lately. The following questions may help:

- What do I think makes a good person? A good action?

- What do I think makes a bad person? A bad action?

5. Create a concrete plan of actions to achieve each goal. That's the essence of writing a goal. Taking into account your abilities, life circumstances, interests and values, begin with one of your current wants and turn it into a plan, with a clear end point so you know when you have achieved the goal. Let us show you how, with the two wants we mentioned above.

"I want to earn more money." Not unreasonable, but not a goal. "I plan to take a computer-skills course at the local technical college so I can apply for a better-paying job." That's more like a

goal, although you should also set sub-goals
to keep you motivated as you work your
way through the course. It will help if you
have some computer ability and you find
working with computers interesting. Notice

> *Don't set goals that depend on someone else's actions.*

that the clear end point is that you apply for a better-paying job,
not that you necessarily get it, because that's outside your control.
Don't set goals that depend on someone else's actions. You may
have done your personal best but miss out for reasons outside
your control. Even if you recognize this, your sense of "failing"
can still squash your motivation. Try to make goals that depend
only on your actions.

"I wish my marriage were more fun." So do many people in a
midlife crisis, but wishing never gets it for them. Try turning this
want into something like this: "I will ask my spouse to go through
the entertainment section of Friday's paper with me to try to find
new common interests we can enjoy together; then I will ask him
to do at least one a week with me." Or how about, "I will ask my
spouse to read a book about improving our sex life with me for at
least half an hour, three times a week, trying out the book's tips as
we go, to give us a more enjoyable sex life." You might have
tackled the same want with a goal like, "I will ask my spouse to go
wife-swapping with me," but unless it conformed with your values
(and your spouse's) it wouldn't be a great idea. (In any case, it
doesn't work. Try a book or videocassette instead.)

We encourage people to set conscious goals for all major areas
of their lives: career, family, friends, learning, recreation, health,
personal development and any others that might be personally
relevant (such as retirement). For the purpose of working your way
out of your midlife crisis, you may want to first try to identify the
life areas that are least rewarding right now. The two that crop up
most commonly for midlife-crisis victims are career and family, but
see which ones seem most important to you and start with those.
Later, if you would like to reduce your vulnerability to anything
like a midlife crisis, we encourage you to complete and continue
goal-setting in your life as a regular part of your lifestyle.

Depression during Menopause

Notice that we are talking about *depression during menopause,* not *menopausal depression*, because the latter does not exist. We realize that idea will surprise a few people, so let us explain. Menopause is a biologically based event, a number of changes occurring in a woman's body triggered by changes in her hormones as she reaches the end of the fertile stage of her life. Some of the symptoms of these biological changes can be disturbing, such as hot flashes, chills, sweats, heart palpitations and headaches. Often, women going through menopause are also depressed, so many assume that this depression is also caused by hormonal changes and so should be called *menopausal depression*.

This explanation makes sense, but it's incorrect. Researchers at Melbourne University in Australia first cast serious doubt on the biological explanation for depression during menopause when they found that there was simply no relationship between a woman's mood level and her hormone levels. Hormone replacement therapy is sometimes used to reduce the effect of the physical symptoms of menopause, for which it is helpful. It was also expected to help with the depression, but it doesn't. Women who suffer from unpleasant or extreme physical symptoms will naturally feel better after those symptoms are relieved, so hormone replacement therapy can *indirectly* help with depression. But it has no direct effect on the mood level of women.

Psychoanalysts (followers of Sigmund Freud) have offered an alternative explanation for "menopausal depression": The depression is triggered by menopause because menopause means the woman can no longer have babies. Like other psychoanalytic ideas, the theory is more complex than that, involving the woman's unresolved sexual conflicts as a result of problems early in life. Like other psychoanalytic ideas, there is no worthwhile evidence to support it.

The final nail in the coffin of menopausal depression came from research by Dr. Marta Frid, a psychologist at La Trobe University in Melbourne. In the first stage of her study, she explored the reasons for the depression occurring in a group of menopausal women. She found significant relationships between their level of depression and five other factors.

1. The loss of a valued role as a homemaker: By the time she reaches menopause, a woman who has made her career as a homemaker inevitably suffers a reduction in the demands and rewards offered by that role. The children are growing up, perhaps have already left home. Her husband has often developed major interests outside the home. There is increasingly less for her to do that she sees as important, with the result that she begins to devalue herself and her achievements.

2. A lack of information about menopause: This problem is often worsened by a belief in popular myths about menopause and its effects. Because of the lack of worthwhile health and human-relations education in years past, some women today still believe that menopause causes obesity, cancer, the end of your sex life, hirsutism (growing hair on your face and body) and even insanity. Expecting events like those would be enough to make anybody depressed!

3. Social isolation resulting in loneliness and a lack of support: This is a common outcome for women who center their lives around a nuclear family, especially those who move to new neighborhoods, away from their extended families.

4. Marital dissatisfaction: Many women can ignore problems or gaps in their marriages while children are at home, providing companionship, needing nurturance and providing access to other social networks, such as parents' groups. As the children leave home, the shortcomings in the marriage become more apparent and have probably gotten worse because of the lack of constructive attention.

5. Economic problems: A common enough source of depression for all of us.

On the other hand, Dr. Frid found no significant relationship between the level of depression and the loss of the ability to have babies, childhood difficulties or the severity of the woman's physiological symptoms of menopause. So much for the biological and psychoanalytic theories of menopausal depression. It obviously makes more sense to talk about depression occurring during menopause, which clearly results from a number of factors, most of which have nothing to do with menopause at all.

This does not deny the reality of menopause, nor the fact that some women will find it physically upsetting and may benefit from appropriate physical treatment. In fact, a lack of information about the real physical effects of menopause does contribute to depression. What Dr. Frid's research shows is that the common causes of depression during menopause are problems occurring in women's lives around that time. The solution to the depression is to do something about those problems.

Dr. Frid used group discussions to give her research subjects accurate information about menopause, anxiety and depression. She encouraged them to discuss women's roles and the need for meaningful activity to build self-esteem. She also encouraged them to identify and discuss the problems in their own lives. By the end of their group program, most of the women had started new rewarding activities, improved their relationships with their husbands and children, and reported a definite sense of improved well-being.

So, the ball's in your court. You may be stuck with menopause, but you are not stuck with depression.

So, the ball's in your court. You may be stuck with menopause, but you are not stuck with depression. The program we have outlined in chapter 10 for managing depression is basically the same as that used in the La Trobe research. Using it as a guide, try to pinpoint the real causes of your depression and do something constructive about them. Also consider setting some goals, as we have explained above.

Although you may have heard the phrase "male menopause" tossed around, there really is no such thing. Men do not have the changes in hormonal function in midlife that women do. What people call male menopause is really a midlife crisis, as we have described it. Similarly, depression during menopause has many of the elements of a midlife crisis, so you may as well look at our suggestions for that, too (starting on page 80).

Like the women in the La Trobe study, you may find it helpful to work on this with the support of other women facing similar issues. If you can't find some friends in the same boat, try your local community center or women's groups (see the Resource section on page 215).

Moving

Moving to a new home is stressful, but being *forced* to move is much more stressful than moving by your own choice. Having to move is a common, recurring stressor for members of the armed services and some branches of public service, but it is also commonly inflicted on the managerial employees of large corporations. Sadly, many of these organizations are inclined to shrug off the problems they are causing their members by saying, "Well, they knew when they took the job that they might have to move. We don't see why they're complaining about it now." If the same organizations were to take a careful look at the number of their experienced members who actually quit, underperform or wind up divorced as a result of forced moves, they might realize they are not managing their human resources very skillfully, at least in this respect.

Wendy Coyle, a researcher at Macquarie University in Sidney, Australia, confirmed American findings on this issue. She found that half of the forced moves she studied were effectively "failures," and half of these were "disasters" that resulted in nervous breakdowns or divorces. A forced move seemed to exaggerate the existing patterns in a marriage. Coyle found that a third of marriages had improved; a third had stayed the same; a third got much worse. She also observed that the effects on children were often ignored or explained away as due to something other than the move. In their desperation to make new friends and be accepted by a new peer group, some children would end up in bad

> *The effects on children were often ignored or explained away as due to something other than the move.*

company and misbehaving. In light of findings like these, there is no doubt that being obligated to move can be a very real life crisis. A company policy of only requesting absolutely necessary moves, of keeping such requests to a minimum, and of providing appropriate support at the time would easily repay any costs involved.

Two other common causes of a forced move are unemployment, which we consider later in this chapter, and separation and divorce, which we consider in chapters 3 and 4. If one of these is the trigger for your unwanted move, take a look at those other discussions as well.

People are sometimes forced to move as a result of having already been victims of another crisis, one that has destroyed their home or made the area unlivable or temporarily dangerous. One group in this situation are refugees, who have often come from crisis experiences that have been severe and prolonged. Many refugees struggle to cope with high levels of stress, frequent relocations after arrival, problems with language and employment, and separation from family members left behind.

Naturally, the situation for those forced to move by some other disaster is worse because for them the crisis of having to move comes on top of the crisis that has taken away their home, sometimes their entire community. Post-disaster relocation may be brief and temporary, eventually followed by a return to the home, but this still adds to the trauma of the crisis and makes it difficult to begin recovery. Or it may be permanent, adding resettlement and readjustment to the crisis already suffered. We consider the specific effects of being the victim of a large-scale crisis in the next chapter, but here we focus on the effects common to all forced moves.

Humans don't cope well with a lot of change. We like the reassurance of the familiar, and we need to feel in control.

Beverley Raphael, professor of psychiatry at the University of Queensland, Australia, has listed the following possible effects of a forced move.

1. The loss of familiar environments and their replacement by a strange environment: Humans don't cope well with a lot of change. We like the reassurance of the familiar, and we need to feel in control. Even desirable changes we have pursued are initially upsetting. This extends to the neighborhood around the home, as well as to the home itself. Even moving to a "better" neighborhood is disruptive at first.

2. The disruption of relationships, both family and social: If you have moved far away, you may completely lose some relationships. Others will be less available to you as sources of support and companionship. In addition to coping with the other effects of the move, you may now be facing the need to find and develop new relationships. That is a process that takes some time for even the most outgoing people. In the meantime, you may suffer a shortage of both support and companionship.

3. Overdependence on family relationships: When you lose your wider circle of relationships, you have to rely more on and spend more time in family relationships, even if only temporarily. This probably accounts for the earlier observation that forced moves tend to exaggerate existing patterns in a marriage. If your marriage is going well, then supporting each other through the stress of the move can strengthen it. Even if your marriage is just okay, it should withstand the additional stress. But if your marriage is already troubled, then the additional stress of a forced move is likely to increase your troubles, and perhaps be the last straw. Similar effects undoubtedly apply to other family relationships, such as parent-child and parent-adolescent relationships.

So, if your present life crisis is being told you must pack your bags and your household and move, what can you do to cope better? The general model of the CRRC applies, even if the crisis of moving doesn't seem as extreme as some of the others in this book. Accept the normality of your reactions and use the suggestions in chapters 7 to 11 to manage them effectively. Especially use the ideas in chapter 9 to give support to

You may be stuck with the move, but you aren't stuck with a crisis.

and gain support from other family members. If the move has brought into focus pre-existing problems in your marriage or family, take the opportunity to tackle those constructively. You can try self-help using other books that pertain specifically to your situation or consult a qualified clinical psychologist or other counselor. You may be stuck with the move, but you aren't stuck with a crisis.

Losing Your Job

You might lose your job because you have been fired or laid off, or because you have retired. Although there are some obvious differences in these causes and in their possible effects on you, the effects also have some things in common. So we will consider them together, pointing out the differences when appropriate.

Our culture places great emphasis on your job as a major part of your identity.

Our culture places great emphasis on your job as a major part of your identity. After we exchange names, the next question is usually "What kind of work do you do?" A job is a badge of your membership in society as a worthwhile citizen, paying her own way. It should give access to rewarding and satisfying activity, and it certainly gives access to pay and the things you buy with it. Having a job gives you status in society, even if different jobs imply different levels of status. It is not surprising that losing your job (or not finding a job) can be a life crisis.

These remarks apply equally to women who have made their career as homemakers. Although many belittle the importance of and demands of being a homemaker, and government doesn't recognize the real contribution of homemakers to our national productivity, it is a valid and socially important career choice and its eventual loss can be just as critical as the loss of any other job. Earlier, in the discussion about depression during menopause, we mentioned that as children grow up and leave home, as the household and sometimes even the house shrink, it is inevitable that the job of the homemaker shrinks, too. It may not disappear as completely as her spouse's job has, but it will gradually become less demanding and rewarding—and less important in her own eyes. Then she, too, faces similar problems as anyone else who has lost his job.

You might see being fired or laid off as evidence of failure on your part and wind up devaluing yourself. We suggest you try to strike a realistic balance in your judgment of the situation. On the one hand, if you can reasonably conclude that you were fired unfairly or laid off for reasons that have nothing to do with your performance, then you might legitimately feel angry at the injustice you have suffered, but you should have no need to blame yourself. On the other hand, if you can accept that in some way you were at fault, that some mistakes or poor performance on your part contributed to the situation, then that at least gives you something concrete to work on. You can take steps to avoid making those mistakes again, or look for a different type of job, or try to improve your performance in your next job, and this will help to restore some sense of being in control of your life.

You may wind up with a mixed interpretation of what has happened. "Sure, I made a few mistakes, but no more than anyone else. It wasn't fair of them to fire me." Fine; you are getting in touch with your feelings and expressing them. That's a good start to coping with your crisis. Just try to interpret the situation as realistically as you can. The suggestions in chapter 8 will help you check the reality of your thoughts about losing your job.

They should also help you with the equally important task of rethinking the role of a job in defining your worth as a human being. We don't want to belittle the value of doing something worthwhile, doing it reasonably well and possibly being paid for it. But there's a lot more to

Even success in the career area of your life does not depend on keeping the job you have just lost.

being a successful human being than just working. If you go back to our discussion of goal-setting above, you will see that "career" is only one of eight suggested important areas in your life. Even success in the career area of your life does not depend on keeping the job you have just lost. There are bound to be other paths to career success for you. Accept the disappointment and possible anger of losing that job, but keep it in perspective.

Most of us don't expect to be fired or laid off, so it's not surprising that we might unfairly interpret the event in self-devaluing ways. All of us expect to retire because, unless you die beforehand or work for yourself, you almost certainly will. Indeed, nowadays early retirement is becoming very popular.

Even though almost everyone will retire at some point, many workers do not prepare themselves well for retirement. Most retirement preparation programs focus on the mechanical and material side, and do not prepare participants for the psychological impact of losing their jobs.

Just as a fired worker may see her job loss as evidence of personal shortcomings, a retiree might interpret his job loss as evidence of being over the hill, too old to do worthwhile work, fit only for the scrap heap. Even if he realizes this is all nonsense, he may still imagine it's what other people think of him. The people who seem most at risk of such misinterpretations are those who have derived most of their sense of personal value from their jobs, perhaps because the job was one with high social status, although not necessarily so. They may also have led imbalanced lifestyles, with little or no other rewarding activity, so they suddenly face big gaps in the day. If they have been ignoring problems in their marriages, the extra time now spent together may bring those to the surface. It's not surprising that many people ill-prepared for retirement tend to die soon after losing their jobs.

Let's get one thing straight about retirement: *It has nothing to do with an older worker's ability to do the job well.* Compulsory retirement was introduced as a social and economic measure to free up jobs for younger workers, not because of any real evidence of significant decline in the abilities of older workers. The reasoning was that older workers would be past the stage of maximum financial need for establishing homes and raising families, so they could be expected to live out the balance of their lives on less income. At a time of restricted job supply, compelling people to retire is meant to give younger people the chance to enter the workforce. You need only look at the ages of many world, community and business leaders to realize that old age is no barrier to doing important tasks well. One of the real effects of compulsory retirement, especially early retirement, has been a massive loss of experience and wisdom from some workplaces.

If your job loss is the result of retirement, we encourage you to interpret that event realistically. In fact, just as more people are now living to an older age, most of them are arriving there in better shape than ever. The popular beliefs that aging inevitably means physical and sexual failure are myths. Of course, we all age physically with real effects, but this *primary aging* is a gradual process that begins early in life and affects all body systems. Many of the problems seen as part of old age are in fact the result of *secondary aging*, caused not by age but by disease, abuse and disuse. These are factors under your control. You can't stop yourself from aging, but you can stop yourself from aging prematurely. It is never too late in life to aim for a more healthy lifestyle, which can be enjoyable in itself and allow you to enjoy the rest of life to the maximum.

> *Many of the problems seen as part of old age are in fact the result of secondary aging, caused not by age but by disease, abuse and disuse.*

Whatever the cause of your job loss, the effect can be a loss of rewarding activities. As we explain in our discussion of depression in chapter 10, you need two kinds of rewards from life to function well: enjoyment and achievement. If you're lucky, your job provides some of both. If you're less fortunate, it will provide some of one of these two rewards. If you're in a real dud of a job, it won't provide much of either kind of reward, although it may at least provide you with the money to gain your rewards through nonjob activities. So, taking care to interpret the reasons for your job loss as realistically as you can, you now need to replace your loss.

We give detailed advice on rebuilding and replacing rewarding activities in chapter 10, as an important part of managing depression. If you are retired, then the suggestions there may be all you need. Go to it! On the other hand, if you are not retired and don't see it as appropriate in your life yet—you may be one of the young unemployed who has not really worked yet—then in addition to those steps in chapter 10, do a job search. You should notice that your job search is *in addition to* building nonjob rewarding activities. By *nonjob* we mean unpaid, and these activities are an important part of a balanced lifestyle, anyway, because they can provide some of the essential rewards that a paying job does not.

Unpaid activities can be even more important for an unemployed person who is searching for a job. Although statistically our unemployment rate is lower than ever, these statistics consider temporary employees as "employed," even though many of these employees will be without work within months, weeks or even days. You may be trying hard to find a permanent job and still miss out. Sure, there are some who take advantage of unemployment programs, but most dislike being on welfare, may even feel ashamed of it, and are trying honestly but unsuccessfully to find a decent job.

The risk in not being hired for a job is almost the same as that in losing a job, that you will misinterpret the event as evidence of your personal shortcomings, see yourself as "failing" in an important area of life, become depressed and give up trying. The truth is, for most job vacancies, there will be more applicants than positions available. This means that some people who could have done the job quite well will not get it. What it does *not* mean is that there is anything wrong with the people who miss out.

The truth is, for most job vacancies, there will be more applicants than positions available.

You may remember that, in the discussion of goal-setting, we advised you to set only goals that depend on *your* actions, not ones that depend on the actions of others, because they are outside your control. You could set a goal of applying for all appropriate jobs. You might increase your chances by presenting yourself as well as possible, perhaps practicing job interviews beforehand. You *will* increase your chances if you present yourself as someone in a good frame of mind with sincere self-confidence, and that's what your nonjob activities can provide. That's why they are important to your job search. We have seen a number of people build their confidence, ward off depression, gain work experience and good work habits by doing volunteer work in between their job applications. The goal you *shouldn't* set is to get a particular job, because that is outside your control. You may present yourself as well as you can, be qualified for the job and still miss out. Instead of giving yourself a well-earned pat on the back for giving it your best shot, you will be telling yourself you "failed" and wondering what is wrong with you. On the strength of a typical job interview, a potential employer doesn't really know you at all, so it makes no sense to see it as a personal rejection.

> *You will increase your chances if you present yourself as someone in a good frame of mind with sincere self-confidence, and that's what your non-job activities can provide.*

We know it is easier said than done, but you should congratulate yourself for achieving your goal of applying for this job and then set your next goal of applying at a different company. In the meantime, those rewarding nonjob activities will help you keep going through this crisis.

6

Coping with Large-Scale Disasters

Large-scale disasters may be natural, such as tornadoes, floods, brushfires or droughts, or they may be man-made, such as airplane or train crashes, sinking ships, building fires, toxic gas leaks or other crises triggered by technological failure or human error. Some crises may involve both elements, such as a plane crash during bad weather or a flood resulting from inadequate flood-control systems. Large-scale disasters can have more potential for trauma than even intense personal disasters. They are often immensely destructive and violent events; they may occupy all of the victim's observable world, surrounding her; and they frequently last for a long time. Not only do they affect each individual victim in the way a personal disaster does, but they also affect her family and other acquaintances, her neighborhood or the whole community. This reduces or removes much of the support that could be available to an individual victim of a personal disaster.

Because large-scale disaster often creates large numbers of victims, post-crisis counseling services may be stretched to their limits and easily overwhelmed. This means that some victims receive little or no supportive counseling, with predictable long-term consequences. Self-help can only strengthen any support you are offered, and it may be the only help you get access to within the critical period after your disaster experience. So we describe the common reactions of victims of large-scale disasters, again with the purpose of helping you to accept the normality of your own reactions and work through them to a successful recovery.

The Stages of a Disaster

Without doubt, Australia's leading expert on the effects of and recovery from disasters is professor of psychiatry Beverley Raphael. While preparing her handbook for the caring professions on the psychology of disaster victims, she thoroughly reviewed the relevant research and we have drawn heavily on her work, especially in this chapter. Professor Raphael first describes seven possible stages of a disaster. This helps us to look at the usual ways victims react at different points during a disaster.

1. **The warning stage:** During this stage, recognizable signs that a disaster may occur are present. For example, there might be weather forecasts or fire warnings, or a breakdown in some safety system that offers no immediate threat but increases vulnerability.

2. **The threat stage:** There are clear indications that a disaster is imminent. These might be flood or tornado warnings, or alarms going off. For some sudden disasters, such as a rail or an air accident, there may have been little or no warning.

3. **The impact stage:** The disaster actually strikes. This might be relatively brief, such as a sudden plane crash, a little longer, such as a tornado or flood, or for a significant length of time, such as a drought or war.

4. **The inventory stage:** Immediately after impact, the victims begin taking stock of the effects of the disaster.

5. **The rescue stage:** Some able victims as well as rescuers from outside the impact zone start to help other victims.

6. **The remedy stage:** More organized and formal attempts are made to help victims.

7. **The recovery stage:** A prolonged period during which the affected community and its individual members readjust and return to equilibrium.

Other researchers have proposed different but basically similar stages. In any particular crisis, some stages may be missing or blurred into others. This scheme fits well with the Crisis Response and Recovery Cycle (CRRC), as we describe in chapter 1, and we use it for following the development of victims' reactions.

Before the disaster

A common reaction to signs of an approaching disaster is apprehension, increasing to anxiety and fear as the inevitability of the disaster becomes clearer. However, a surprising number of people shrug off even clear warnings. As we discuss in chapter 1, early in life we come to believe that crises won't happen to us, a belief that is a delusion but that helps us function normally. Some people begin to prepare, especially if they have previously experienced similar disasters. On the other hand, if past warnings were not followed by disasters, many people are understandably if regrettably less likely to heed a new warning.

Glorianne Swift, an employee of the Darwin Bureau of Meteorology and survivor of Cyclone Tracy, which hit northern Australia in 1974, said that, like most Darwin residents, she was indifferent about tornados before Tracy. "When we heard there was a tornado coming, we'd think of filling the bath up with ice, stuffing the refrigerator with beer—and let's have a party." It seems that preparations, even in areas of obviously high but uncertain risk, are often not carried out, perhaps because they cause inconvenience and people refuse to believe they are at real risk. As a result, when clear warnings are issued, they often go to people who are basically unprepared. This can intensify their shock and later lead to anger at the authorities for not giving "adequate" warnings.

For their part, authorities are sometimes reluctant to issue warnings until the risk is high, out of fear of issuing either a false alarm or one that is too early and has lost its impact by the time the disaster does occur. In fact, research on this issue tends to discount both of these possibilities. Residents of Los Angeles, who had to live for months in 1977 and 1978 with the threat of an impending major earthquake, generally showed no adverse effects and some increasingly adaptive behavior. Nonetheless, the period of waiting for the impact of a disaster, after all preparations have been done, is often one of rising tension and fear.

After a disaster, those who survived at least partly because of their preparations sometimes make light of their actions. Most of us tend to be a bit overmodest about our achievements, but in this case the prepared survivors may also fear the envy of those who suffered more, even if they suffered because of their own lack of preparation. For their part, survivors who ignored warnings and made no preparations are likely to be self-blaming and self-critical of themselves afterward, with the risk of increasing their depression.

The way an individual responds, before and during a crisis, is strongly influenced by whether he has an immediate family. Much of a victim's thoughts and behavior become focused on his family, on attempts to be with them, to protect them, to check their safety or at least to communicate. If possible, families try to meet before a disaster strikes and plan how to cope together. Charles Capewell was a passenger with his two sons on British Airways Flight 009 on June 24, 1982, when it lost power in all four engines after flying into a cloud of volcanic dust and smoke over Indonesia. As the plane lost height and the crew desperately tried to restart the engines, Mr. Capewell took out his airline ticket and scribbled a note on the cover: "Ma. In trouble. Plane going down. Will do best for boys. We love you. Sorry. Pa. XXX." He then wrapped the ticket and his passport in a plastic bag and put it inside his sweater.

The way an individual responds, before and during a crisis, is strongly influenced by whether he has an immediate family.

Before the disaster is imminent, its threat actually generates a great deal of excitement and arousal, with heightened activity. Normal activities, such as work or school, may be abandoned as attention is focused on pre-disaster preparations. All of this can be accompanied by feeling alert, high, even good, especially for children and adolescents. This excitement may even continue right through a relatively nonthreatening crisis. Afterward, victims can feel guilty for having felt good about an event that has caused suffering or destruction. Paul Grigson, a journalist, was on the United Airlines Flight 811 that suffered a massive blow-out in its cabin fuselage in February 1989, causing nine people to be sucked out of the aircraft to their deaths and making the plane extremely difficult to control. After the pilot made a successful emergency landing at Honolulu, Mr. Grigson slid down the escape chute and then walked toward the front of the plane, only then realizing how much damage had been done and that people had died. He later wrote, "My adventure had turned to tragedy, my calmness to stupidity, my bravado about having made it to an embarrassed feeling of insensitivity."

In most situations, as the disaster draws near, the excitement is replaced by fear. Strangely enough, experts in the field all observe that panic is unusual, despite the Hollywood image of disasters. Betty Tootell, another passenger on British Airways Flight 009, who later wrote a book about her experience, observed there was remarkably little panic as the powerless plane descended. Most passengers sat quietly, while some suddenly felt it was important to exchange names. Dr. Jack Kennedy and his sons, Richard and John, were also on the United Airlines Flight 811 that suffered a cabin blow-out. Richard later said, "When I saw people grabbing life vests, I knew there was something seriously wrong. Everyone was surprisingly calm about it. Nobody was really panicking."

Strangely enough, experts in the field all observe that panic is unusual, despite the Hollywood image of disasters.

Some survivors afterward report having had "omens" or "signs" of the impending disaster. They may describe a warning dream or the day of the disaster seeming somehow different. From a psychologist's point of view, these are really examples of how human memory is selective and interpreted in the light of our present circumstances, rather than evidence of anything supernatural or extrasensory. It also probably represents a common theme of the recovery cycle: the attempt to make sense of your crisis and regain some sense of control.

During the disaster

The immediate effect of the disaster will be shock, all the more intense if there has been little or no warning. At first, some people may misinterpret the nature of an unwarned disaster: for example, mistaking the noise of a tornado for bombing. Mistakes like these are more common when a disaster occurs at night, when victims feel more disoriented and isolated. Disasters may involve extremely strong sensations—sights, sounds and movements—that can imprint powerful memories in the minds of survivors. Ms. Swift, a survivor of Cyclone Tracy, described looking out the window and seeing trees slashed by rain and doubled over. Then the lights went out and the phone went dead. Later, when she went to the kitchen to get her husband, David, a beer, she opened the door and found everything gone. The wind and rain had been so fierce that the family had not heard their kitchen and dining room being torn apart. Their stove had been blown into the neighbor's backyard and their refrigerator had disappeared. It was then that they took shelter in their basement.

Fear is the natural response, and can help focus your mind on ways to survive, yet it is often misperceived as a sign of weakness and inadequacy.

Professor Raphael has described the common pattern of emotional reactions during the impact of a disaster. A typical victim experiences heightened arousal, extreme alertness, with a focus on survival, for himself and his family or group. Although the fear is intense, there is usually little panic. Fear is the natural response and can help focus your mind on ways to survive, yet it is often misperceived as a sign of weakness and inadequacy. If the forces of the disaster are strong, victims may feel helpless, especially during a prolonged disaster. Some people feel abandoned, when it seems they have been forsaken, even by their gods. One expert believes this is a major part of the emotional distress during the impact of a disaster, especially affecting children who are separated from their parents. Many develop an intense yearning for escape or rescue. People who may not have prayed for years will do so, sometimes attempting to "bargain": "Let me escape, God, and I will be a better person afterward."

The most obvious action to take during impact is to try to escape, if that is possible, and most victims make this their first response. Again, this is usually not a reaction of blind panic, but a more or less reasoned attempt, even if associated with extreme fear. Some people are paralyzed by fear and may start trying to escape only when they see others trying to escape. If escape is impossible, victims may adopt protective postures, such as hiding behind or under something, and curling up their bodies. People frequently hold on to others, for mutual support or to try to protect weaker loved ones. As previously mentioned, behavior during a disaster becomes focused on the family, and fear and arousal can become intense if a person is separated from family members.

Heroic actions occur during the impact, although more so later. Some people go to remarkable lengths to try to help others, even strangers. Unfortunately, some heroic attempts at rescue are foolhardy and may end tragically. As we have pointed out, true *panic*—utterly disorganized behavior marked by a loss of control—is rare. It seems more likely to occur in a few already vulnerable people, and in circumstances when victims lack communication with others and do not know what to expect, how long the disaster may last or whether any help is nearby. Uncertainty, confusion and helplessness all increase the risk of panic. If you are now remembering an episode of panic, do not interpret these findings unrealistically as evidence of your inadequacy. Keep in mind the normality of all these reactions, and that they vary from person to person.

Researchers have described a pattern of reactions, technically called the *disaster syndrome*, that can occur during impact or immediately afterward. A victim with this syndrome appears dazed, stunned, apathetic and passive, possibly sitting or standing still or wandering aimlessly. She may seem unaware of her surroundings, possible dangers or the presence or needs of others. This reaction has been observed in 20 to 25 percent of the victims of a severe disaster. Before long, it is usually replaced by activity, which can be agitated, although the shock sometimes lasts for several hours. During this time the person may need protection.

One study of victims' reactions during a crisis found three main groups: 12 to 25 percent were "cool and collected"; 50 to 75 percent were "stunned and bewildered"; and 10 to 25 percent showed extreme responses such as panic, paralysis or hysteria.

Another researcher found that 70 percent of disaster victims were unable to think as well as usual; 25 percent behaved strangely, sometimes freezing; 33 percent showed some leadership; 47 percent cooperated with others; 22 percent made major rescue attempts. Other researchers have observed the physiological reactions we describe in chapter 1, such as a pounding heart, tense muscles, pains, fainting, headaches and diarrhea. Once again we draw to your attention how the norm is to *react strongly.*

The way a victim behaves during impact can have a big influence on his later recovery. People tend to review and evaluate how they acted during a crisis, with the risk that they judge themselves in unfairly negative ways. When victims replay in their minds their crisis behavior, it must either fit with their view of themselves, or their view of themselves must change.

The way a victim behaves during impact can have a big influence on his later recovery.

Victims' experience of time is also distorted. For some it passes quickly, with an incident over seemingly as soon as it began. For others it passes slowly. Some victims talk later of things happening "in slow motion." If the disaster does go on for any length of time, victims tend to focus on when it will end. They may reach points of believing they can go on no longer, although most then find new strength if they need to. And, finally, it does end.

After the disaster

At first, people may not believe their crisis is over, but as they do accept it, most are slowly filled with relief and joy. Often people feel a great sense of personal power at having survived, having beaten the crisis. Identification with fellow survivors can add to this feeling, and the mutual support they share increases it. Survivors can express their relief in many ways: being quiet, feeling elated, actively rejoicing, even dancing. Some begin talking about their experiences, trying to make sense of them.

As the British Airways Flight 009 finally made a safe landing on three restarted engines at Jakarta Airport, in Indonesia, there was first a moment of almost incredulous silence, followed by

> *Often people feel a great sense of personal power at having survived, having beaten the crisis.*

a burst of applause. Duty-free alcohol and cigarettes were passed around with abandon and that night parties went on until dawn.

But also there is an increasing realization of the extent of injury and destruction, including personal injury, as victims take inventory of what happened to them. Shock, or the disaster syndrome, may serve to protect people at this stage from the full enormity of the disaster. The release of stress can also be expressed physiologically, with the same kinds of reactions as described earlier. One researcher found these physical symptoms had occurred in two-thirds of survivors. Fear, anxiety and high arousal may also continue, despite the release of tension. It was observed that more than 90 percent of survivors began to experience anxiety again within five hours of rescue. It often set in when they slowed down, by going to bed or stopping other activities. Those victims who had been most severely exposed to the disaster were the ones who suffered the most anxiety later. A passenger on the United Airlines Flight 811, who had been surprised by her calmness during the midair crisis, awoke that night in tears in her hotel room.

In working through their recovery, victims of large-scale disasters follow similar patterns to those we describe in chapter 1, including a lot of mental review. Many of the survivors of the British Airways Flight 009 say their experience, which lasted only twelve minutes, has permanently affected their lives. They formed a club for fellow survivors, which has regular reunions. Billie Walker, the club's founding secretary, said, "Everything is far more in perspective now . . . each day is a bonus and all the problems you normally have in your life don't seem nearly as desperate."

June Bellairs said, "It made me appreciate life. Even simple things, like birds and trees, you know. You take things like that for granted until something like this happens."

In the immediate aftermath of a large-scale disaster, there is usually a massive response of rescue and support, although Professor Raphael observes that this often focuses on medical and material support, to the neglect of psychological support. Communities may become more united as they struggle together to recover. Debbie Fleming was a resident of a small town in Victoria, Australia, during the Ash Wednesday brushfires of 1983 that killed seven residents and destroyed hundreds of homes. She described how the community rallied together in a way she had never witnessed before, even though she had lived there all her life.

Communities may become more united as they struggle together to recover.

Public interest in a large-scale disaster can wane quickly, and with it public support. Victims often face long-term problems from forced relocation, temporary living facilities, pursuing insurance claims, rebuilding and so on. Ms. Fleming's former neighbors moved away and eventually divorced. In any case, a successful recovery means diminishing the crisis experience to just a painful memory. Ms. Fleming describes how the heightened communal spirit she encountered slowly dissipated. Cyclone Tracy survivor Glorianne Swift describes how the hairs on the back of her neck stand on end now when she hears the tornado warning siren, but otherwise she and her family are settled back in their rebuilt and now tornado-proof home. Mark Weiss is a Mississippi farmer whose property is subject to recurrent flooding, so much so that he and his family now have a standard routine for evacuating their children and removing equipment and valuable possessions to safety. Like other people who live in hazard-prone areas, he has developed both a sensible plan of preparation and a philosophical acceptance of the risks and costs involved.

Natural versus Man-Made Disasters

Dr. Andrew Baum is professor of medical psychology at the Uniformed Services University of the Health Sciences, in Maryland. He has made a study of the differences in effects of natural versus man-made disasters and has concluded that the man-made variety can cause more severe and longer-lasting problems. He gives several reasons for this.

- Survivors of man-made disaster may become involved in court cases seeking compensation. No one would deny they have certain rights, but such court cases are often both delayed and prolonged. This can result in the survivors having to relive their crisis experiences when they finally come to court, and meanwhile being prevented from regarding the crisis as finally over.

- While we don't expect to control nature, we prefer to think we control our technology. A technological disaster can therefore reduce our feelings of control more than a natural one would. Much of the impact of a crisis comes from its blow to our sense of control, and much of the recovery cycle is aimed at regaining that sense.

- Most natural disasters arrive quickly, strike fiercely and then depart. They tend to reach their lowest point pretty quickly. Many man-made disasters do not have such clear beginnings and endings. For example, a nuclear reactor or chemical plant can leak for some time before possible victims learn they are at risk. There may be some doubt as to when the contamination and risks are really gone. This is particularly true when the disaster has involved exposure to toxic substances, the effects of which may not emerge for years.

- The responsible authorities tend to lose credibility as a result of man-made disasters, because they may be seen as allowing the crisis to occur in the first place. When they try to offer reassurances that the crisis is over or that there will be no long-term effects, people are less inclined to believe them.

Dr. Baum and his colleagues compared people living near a toxic waste dump with victims of a flood and found those living near the dump were more distressed. Those near the dump also showed stress problems similar to people who lived near the Three Mile Island nuclear reactor when it suffered a major malfunction and leaked radioactive material.

Post-Traumatic Stress Disorders

Some disaster victims' crisis reactions become ingrained or keep reappearing in a severe and disruptive way. This is the problem now known as *post-traumatic stress disorder*. Although this disorder has been commonly observed and studied in combat veterans, in fact it can occur in any crisis victim. It includes the following factors:

- The victim has experienced an identifiable situation that would cause symptoms of distress in anyone.

- The victim keeps experiencing the event over again, through recurring and intrusive memories or dreams, or by feeling or acting as though the event were happening again.

- The victim shows reduced responsiveness to and involvement in the world, beginning some time after the crisis.

- The victim shows at least two of the following symptoms after the crisis: extreme alertness and a tendency to react in a startled way; disturbed sleep; guilt about surviving; memory or concentration problems; avoidance of situations that might remind her of the crisis; an increase in any of these symptoms when reminded of the crisis, even symbolically.

Crises that were extremely stressful, that involved a serious personal threat and an intense shock effect, and in which the victim felt helpless, are more likely to produce reactions similar to those of post-traumatic stress disorder. Whether these reactions develop into the full-blown disorder depends in part on how psychologically vulnerable the victim was before the crisis. It also depends on whether victims receive adequate supportive counseling during the critical six weeks after the crisis.

Your Recovery

Because you are reading this now, you have probably already been through your crisis experience and are working on your recovery. Good for you. No matter how much, or how little, support you receive from others, ultimately your recovery is in your own hands, as is the solution to all psychological problems. Others can help, and we hope this book does, but only *you* can do it. We suggest you remember two points from the above description of victims' reactions to large-scale disasters.

First, normal human beings tend to have intense emotional and physical reactions of a wide variety when involved in a large-scale disaster. That's normal. Second, the CRRC fits this situation well, which means our suggestions in chapters 7 to 11 should be helpful. It is also not unusual for victims of large-scale crises to have faced death, the risk of their own or the actuality of others', or to have been forced to relocate, temporarily or permanently. The destruction of homes or entire communities may mean making a completely new start in major life areas. You will therefore find helpful suggestions in some of the other chapters as well.

Preparing for Crises

We cannot avoid the fact that most ordinary people do not prepare themselves specifically for coping with possible disasters, even when there is good reason to believe they are at risk. This is probably for the same reason people ignore explicit warnings of an imminent disaster: We don't want to believe it could happen to us. To prepare for a possible disaster is to admit it could happen to us.

To prepare for a possible disaster is to admit it could happen to us.

Teaching basic first-aid and resuscitation to the general community is still possible and desirable. Immediately after the impact of some disasters, before rescue teams can arrive from outside the disaster area, many survivors will be in a position to offer immediate assistance to other survivors. Indeed, as the research we mention above shows, many *do* attempt rescues and other helpful acts. The more survivors who know basic first-aid and emergency resuscitation, the more effective those attempts will be. Because first-aid and even resuscitation are not directly linked with the idea of disaster, they should be less threatening to ordinary people.

Community disaster-preparation programs should continue and be expanded, because there are always some people willing to face their risks more realistically. In times of crisis, they can provide examples of constructive reaction and leadership that will reduce the risk of panic. No matter how much the general community is encouraged to increase its self-help capacity, when it comes down to it, we are very dependent on our trained emergency services.

There is simply no substitute for live practice of emergency procedures, under the most realistic conditions possible. Such rehearsals can reduce the shock impact of a real crisis, test procedures and equipment, and build the confidence of emergency workers to handle themselves competently in hazardous situations. These practice runs need to occur frequently enough to maintain an acceptable level of readiness. Obviously, that costs money. So does the long-term therapy of someone suffering from an unresolved crisis reaction or worse, a post-traumatic stress disorder. Professor Raphael observes that most community disaster plans are able to cope with large numbers of physical casualties but are rarely able to meet the psychological needs of victims.

Rescuers Can Be Victims

A possibility often overlooked or actively denied is the risk of a
crisis reaction in the rescuers who go into a disaster area after the
initial impact. Many assume that because rescuers miss the impact,
or sometimes because rescue is seen as part of their job, they are
not affected in the way the actual victims are. This assumption is
clearly false.

When Swiss Air Flight 111 crashed off Peggy's Cove in Nova
Scotia, Paul Porter, a member of the Coast Guard, expected to help
survivors but ended up gathering debris and remains from the
ocean. He still struggles with nightmares and reminders of the
incident: His wife eventually moved a painting of an historic
Peggy's Cove lighthouse out of their living room.

Even though rescuers usually miss
the actual impact of the disaster, they
may have more prolonged and closer
contact with its effects. They may have
to fight fires, search through rubble for
victims, or be repeatedly confronted by
injury and death. Because they see
themselves in a vital and supportive role,
they may try to suppress their own feelings. Major disasters can
make enormous demands on their personal resources, producing
fatigue and reducing their ability to cope. With supportive services
focusing on the immediate victims, the real needs of rescuers may
go unnoticed and unmet.

> *Even though rescuers
> usually miss the actual
> impact of the disaster,
> they may have more
> prolonged and closer
> contact with its effects.*

Critical-incident stress debriefing

Recognizing that rescuers, including those from our professional
emergency services, can easily become victims themselves should
lead us to accept the need for both adequate preparation before
crises and adequate support after a crisis. Professor Jeffrey Mitchell,
whose work we mention earlier in the book, has developed a
procedure for providing this support.

The goals of critical-incident stress debriefing are, first, to
protect and support the personnel involved in the incident and,

second, to avoid abnormal and exaggerated stress responses. The debriefing process can occur at four points.

On-scene or near-scene debriefing is usually done by an officer or manager in the service involved, or it can be done by a chaplain or professional counselor. Essentially he talks with the personnel during their breaks, providing emotional support mostly by listening and showing acceptance of their stress reactions. He also monitors each person's present state, deciding when an emergency worker should be taken out for a longer break.

The *initial defusing* should occur within a few hours of the incident and also is usually led by an officer from the service. It can be led by a professional counselor or it may develop spontaneously as workers are stowing gear or packing up. Initial defusing is basically an opportunity for workers to talk about their feelings and reactions in an unstructured way. It is essential that this is done in a supportive atmosphere with no criticism of anyone's actions or reactions. The time for formal reviews of performance and procedures is later.

The formal debriefing should occur between twenty-four and forty-eight hours after the incident. Any sooner, and some workers will not yet be ready to talk openly; any longer, as we have mentioned, the less effective it becomes and the higher the risk of some workers having long-term problems. Because strong feelings may emerge during this session, it is best led by a professional counselor. An untrained discussion leader may be overwhelmed by the strength of some reactions, be unable to guide the group's interactions in helpful ways and actually do more harm than good.

The formal debriefing usually takes from three to five hours, and goes through six phases. First, during the *introductory phase*, the leader sets the guidelines for the meeting. At this point, the leader should emphasize the confidentiality of what will be discussed, so that group members feel free to be open without fear of any backlash from outsiders. Second, during the *fact phase*, members gradually build up a literal description of the incident by each describing her own experiences, adding to the complete picture. Third, during the feeling phase, group members add their emotional reactions to the description of the event. Fourth, during the symptom phase, group members are asked to describe anything unusual they experienced during the crisis or since. This gives them an opportunity to describe their stress reactions in their own words. Fifth, during the teaching phase, the group leader explains the CRRC, as we describe it in chapter 1. He emphasizes the normality and variability of the human stress response to a crisis. Finally, during the re-entry phase, the group wraps up any loose ends in the discussion. Sometimes this involves planning future action.

The *follow-up debriefing* occurs several weeks or months after the crisis, if it is needed. Its purpose is to tackle any unresolved issues left over, which may be indicated by one or more workers not progressing through a satisfactory recovery cycle. It may need to be done with one worker, a few, or the whole group, and it may require a number of sessions. This debriefing is really the transition from counseling to therapy and, as such, should only be attempted by qualified professional counselors.

The critical-incident-stress-debriefing process can look deceptively simple but that should not lead you to underestimate its effectiveness, if done with appropriate timing and skill. Experts believed stress debriefing would prevent crisis victims from developing more serious problems later, such as post-traumatic stress disorder. More recent research suggests this is not true. The main benefits of debriefing are to provide relief and support and to contribute to the morale of the group or organization. Other factors, particularly personal vulnerability and the overall atmosphere of the organization, are more important determinants of long-term risk.

> *The main benefits of debriefing are to provide relief and support and to contribute to the morale of the group or organization.*

This research also has important implications for the formal debriefing described above. In the past, some counselors have emphasized the expression of feelings at this stage, which involves almost reliving the event. This now seems not only unnecessary but possibly harmful by adding a second traumatic experience to the first. In light of this, if you find yourself involved in critical-incident stress debriefing, we suggest you adapt Professor Mitchell's procedure along these lines:

- Keep the meetings brief, just long enough to get things done.

- Be flexible in your approach and agenda, tailoring it to the needs of your group and the specific situation.

- Encourage participants to support each other, at the time and later.

- Keep the focus of the discussion on education about the CRRC and ways to foster mutual, practical support, rather than just revisiting the original experience.

- For a reasonable period after the event, monitor anyone who seems vulnerable. A rule of thumb is that adverse reactions often appear three weeks later.

Intelligent and cost-effective management of human resources begins with recognizing everyone's humanity. Any organization whose members have a significant risk of being involved in crises would find that the investment in adequate preparation and support more than repays itself.

7

Coping with Any Crisis

The opportunity to do something practical to cope with a life crisis will usually occur during the recovery stage. Many crises are too brief or too traumatic for victims to do anything more than react with the crisis response (see chapter 1). However, you may have an opportunity to begin some practical steps during a long-term crisis, such as a life-threatening illness, a major conflict within an important relationship or the impending death of someone close.

Many crises have clear time boundaries. A fire begins, burns and then is extinguished. An accident occurs, trapping you in some wreckage, then you are released and taken to the hospital. You are assaulted for about twenty minutes but then escape from your attacker. The situation that has caused your emotional upheaval has a definite ending and you are faced with the task of recovery. But some life crises are not so clear, at least not their conclusions. When coping with the prolonged illness and eventual death of someone close, many people will work through a lot of their grief before the eventual death, which may be welcomed, in a way, as a release from suffering. Some of the life-stage crises we discuss in chapter 5 may have no obvious end point. Is your midlife crisis over when you reach fifty? Or, more realistically, is it over when you have come to terms with it? Does the crisis of being laid off end when you find another job? Because you may not; instead, you may resolve the situation by eventually seeing yourself as retired.

During these lengthier crises, the major emotional response will occur when you first become aware of the situation: being told your parent has terminal cancer, or being forced into early retirement or whatever the initial event is. The crisis response—the state of intense emotional reaction to the situation—usually does not last more than four to six weeks, even though a clear release from the crisis may not come until some time later. You will probably have begun the process of recovery before that, even if you cannot complete it until that later release.

So the point at which you can start trying our suggestions for coping with and recovering from your crisis will depend on several factors. If you have suffered a brief or traumatic crisis, gone through the usual reactions of shock, denial, realization and non-emotional survival, then you probably aren't able even to think about coping or recovery until after your "escape." On the other hand, if you are coping with a long-term crisis, you may be able to contemplate taking some practical steps as your initial intense reaction diminishes, even though you have not yet escaped from the crisis situation itself.

Your ability to start some practical action will also depend on your awareness of what you might do. Few of us are prepared for our life crises and so we may be stuck for ideas, even when our ability to act begins to return. You may need to be prompted by this book, a friend, relative or counselor. The point is, the sooner your level of emotional arousal and your awareness of practical possibilities allow you to start taking some practical steps, the better. A basic plan for coping with and recovering from a crisis is detailed in the box opposite.

A Basic Plan for Coping with a Crisis

1. Understand and accept your stress reactions as normal (review chapter 1).

2. Share your feelings constructively (see chapter 8).

3. Get your life organized again.

4. Find and use helpful resources (see this chapter and chapter 8).

5. Use drugs as a temporary aid, if at all.

6. Manage any strong emotional reactions (see chapters 8 and 10).

7. Manage any physical reactions, such as disturbed sleep (see chapter 9) or diarrhea (see your doctor).

8. Eventually come to terms with your crisis and lay it to rest (see chapters 1, 7 and 8).

Accept Your Normal Reactions

First, understand and accept your reactions, both emotional and physical, as normal reactions to a crisis. We cannot emphasize this point enough. The Crisis Response and Recovery Cycle (CRRC) are the normal reactions of humans to the major disruption of a crisis. To have these reactions means you are normal. *Not* to have some reactions like these would be unusual and would likely signal the beginning of problems. Review our description of the Crisis Response and Recovery Cycle in chapter 1 and accept the normality of how this cycle plays out in your situation.

Also remember our emphasis on the normal *variability* of human reactions to crisis. We have widened our focus to include all kinds of life crises, not only the traumatic or life-threatening ones, so many readers will normally experience other emotional reactions as well. If you see your crisis as an intense threat, you may experience anxiety. If you see your crisis as a major loss, you may be more likely to experience grief, deprivation or mourning. If you see your crisis as a challenge, you may experience some excitement or hope as you try to grapple with it. If your crisis involves important relationships, you may experience anger, frustration, hurt or even hatred.

Our working definition of a crisis is that it is any event that causes you to experience unusually strong emotions, strong enough to interfere with your ability to function. The specific emotions you experience will reflect the nature of the crisis, your perceptions of it, your own psychological makeup and your immediate situation. Whatever they may be, having strong emotions in response to a crisis is normal. Practical suggestions to help you accept and manage your emotional reactions are in chapter 8.

> *The specific emotions you experience will reflect the nature of the crisis, your perceptions of it, your own psychological makeup and your immediate situation.*

Share Your Feelings

After you accept your feelings as normal, share them constructively. You do not have a choice *whether* you share your feelings, only *how* you share them. You express most of your feelings nonverbally—you give off "vibes"—and you have little control over this. If your vibes tell someone you feel bad, but you say nothing or even deny you feel bad, then you are sending two messages: 1) "I feel bad" and 2) "But I won't/can't talk about it." You may then lose the vital emotional support of those who care about you.

The other mistake is to express your feelings *destructively*, by dumping them on someone else in a blaming or aggressive way. Again, you might be losing some important support. Try to share your feelings constructively, in ways that leave you feeling better but do not threaten your important relationships. You will find advice for sharing your feelings constructively in chapter 9.

Group sharing

If you belong to a group that is involved in the crisis together—a family, a work team, a local community—it can be helpful if someone initiates the chance for the members of the group to share their feelings. One or more of the group members, a leader of some kind or a counselor may open up and lead the discussion. Group discussions like these are more likely to be helpful if everyone agrees, at the beginning, that everything discussed is confidential, that no one may mention an individual's statements outside the group in a way that could identify that person. Knowing that what she says will be kept confidential can help someone open up about issues that she may otherwise keep bottled up.

Knowing that what she says will be kept confidential can help someone open up about issues that she may otherwise keep bottled up.

If possible, several such group meetings should be conducted, at different stages after the crisis and for different purposes. Within a few hours of the crisis, group members or a designated leader can conduct an *initial defusing*. Group members are encouraged to talk about their feelings and reactions to the crisis. This must be done within a positive and supportive atmosphere, with an emphasis on care and concern for group members. This is not the time to criticize or evaluate anyone's behavior during the crisis, and no one should be criticized for how he feels. This meeting usually lasts about an hour.

Between twenty-four and forty-eight hours after the crisis, a *formal stress debriefing* should be held. Many people are not ready to participate any sooner than twenty-four hours because they are still experiencing the natural reactions of shock or denial. The longer you wait beyond forty-eight hours, however, the less effective a stress debriefing becomes until, six weeks later, it is ineffective. Again, this does not mean you can't do something effective for a group later if nothing was done within the first six weeks—your group meeting will just need to be more long-term and therapeutic to begin undoing any problems that have accumulated since the crisis.

In either case, whether the group can meet soon or must wait until later, someone trained in both group dynamics and crisis counseling should lead the meetings. Unstructured group meetings, led by people who may have good intentions but no appropriate training, can be not only unhelpful but actually harmful to participants. A trained group leader will guide the naturally developing group processes in helpful directions and keep the group from straying in harmful ones. A trained crisis counselor will make sure the group covers the appropriate content in its discussions, neither omitting anything desirable nor including anything undesirable. For the most effective stress debriefings, you need a facilitator who can fill both roles. If your group meetings have been delayed and must now serve a therapeutic role as well, then it is essential that someone with appropriate qualifications, such as a clinical psychologist, lead the meetings. As we discuss in chapter 6, Professor Mitchell has proposed a plan for stress debriefings. The opportunity to conduct them is more likely to arise with high-risk groups, such as emergency service personnel (see page 113).

> *Unstructured group meetings, led by people who may have the best of intentions but no appropriate training, can be not only unhelpful but actually harmful to participants.*

Get Organized

The next step is to get organized again. One of the major effects of a crisis is disorganization. The sudden and unexpected nature of the crisis and the intensity of your normal reactions disrupt your usual living routines. In the case of a brief crisis, that disruption may not matter, except to the extent that it carries over into and interferes with your recovery. In the case of a long-term crisis, an ongoing disruption of your living routines may become an additional source of stress in itself, reducing your ability to cope with the crisis situation. Then the question becomes, what practical steps can you take to restore as much of your normal living routines as is possible under the circumstances of the crisis?

Do you need to make some arrangements for accommodation? Food? Clothing? Financial support? Work? Transportation? Medical treatment? Nursing care? Insurance? Like all of us, you have limited amounts of energy and time to handle life's demands. Now you have an extra demand: either recovering from your immediate past crisis or coping with an ongoing crisis.

So you need to put some thought into how to use your resources most efficiently. Try making a list of everything you need or want to do and then go through the list ranking each item according to priority. It doesn't matter if you can't differentiate among all of them. What you need is a classification, such as "urgent and important," "desirable but not essential" and "postponable." Then you can take care of the urgent and important tasks first, moving next to some of the desirable but not essential ones. If anything does have to wait until you are under less pressure, at least it will be something you have decided was less essential or even postponable.

Use Your Resources

As a part of getting your life organized again, whether coping with an ongoing crisis or working through recovery, you should identify and use the resources available to you. We don't mean your inner resources. We offer you suggestions for strengthening and using those in chapters 8 and 10. Right now we want you to look for and get support from the resources around you. These might be people, organizations or objects.

Several times we have mentioned the valuable emotional support you can get from friends and relatives. *Helpful emotional support means they are willing to listen to you describe your feelings and reactions and then show that they accept the normality of what you are describing.* This helps you to accept and express your reactions. Can you think of who will do that for you? Don't be afraid to ask for this kind of help. A crisis can occur in anyone's life at any time. The person you are leaning on now may be glad of your relationship and the support you can offer when she has her crisis next year.

You might wear out your welcome if you depend too much on just one other listener, so try to find several. You might also wear out your welcome if you keep going over the same ground.

> *You might wear out your welcome if you depend too much on just one other listener, so try to find several.*

This should not happen if you are progressing normally through your recovery cycle. Some review of the crisis is normal during recovery, as you come to terms with it. If you think you may be getting stuck and going over the same ground too much, you may be able to get yourself unstuck using the suggestions in chapter 8 or you may decide to seek some professional help. In the meantime, let your friends say for themselves whether they are sick of listening to you.

✗ Be selective in your use of emotional support. We have defined helpful emotional support above. *Unhelpful* emotional support means someone is encouraging you to either deny your feelings or exaggerate them. People who tell you to "Forget all about it" or "Put it all behind you now" or "Stop making a fuss

> *Unhelpful emotional support means someone is encouraging you to either deny your feelings or exaggerate them.*

about it" may themselves be suffering from the "John Wayne syndrome" ("You're not hurt unless a bone is showing"). Or your distress is so uncomfortable for them they want you to keep it to yourself. Or they may believe they are truly helping you get over your crisis more quickly. Whatever their motives, if they encourage you to deny and bottle up your normal stress reactions, they are doing you no favors at all. If someone you want or need to maintain contact with responds this way, tell him you appreciate his attempts to be helpful, but that you would find it even more helpful if he would just listen to and accept what you say about how you are feeling. If it's not someone you want or need to maintain contact with, see less of him, at least for the time being.

On the other hand, emotional support that encourages you to *exaggerate* your bad feelings is no help either. If your friend or relative wants to show how much she cares by getting even angrier than you about what happened, you may have a good hate session but not get much further, especially if she encourages you to develop and nurse a grudge. Some people believe it is always helpful to listen to a distressed person rehearse his problems, no matter how often he has done so before. If you are getting stuck in your post-crisis depression instead of working through it, then the friend who always offers a sympathetic ear may unintentionally encourage you to stay stuck. If you think you have told your story of woe too many times and your friend hasn't mentioned it, then maybe it's time you said to yourself, "Yes, it is understandable and sad that you are depressed about what happened to you. What are you now thinking of doing about your depression?"

Some people get high on a crisis; they like the urgency and excitement. If they can't have one of their own, they might want to share yours. As a result, they may encourage you to dwell on it unnecessarily. If you are going over your crisis experience again because it is helping you come to terms with it, that's fine. But if you are reliving it for someone else's benefit, be wary—you might be giving yourself another dose of depression. Be willing to say, "Thanks for your interest and support, but I'd rather not discuss it now."

Or they may want to tell you what to do. Friends and relatives can be important resources for practical help as well as emotional support. Can someone lend you some money? Cover your job? Help out with the kids? Do some shopping? If so, fine. Figure out what you need, identify someone to ask and again don't talk yourself out of making reasonable requests for practical help.

> *Be wary of people who want you to do what they have decided.*

This is quite different from someone telling you *what* to do. We are suggesting you identify your needs for assistance and then ask for help—to do what *you* have decided. Be wary of people who want you to do what *they* have decided.

We don't mean to discourage you from asking for advice. If you aren't sure what to do, or how to tackle some problem, by all means ask someone that you think may be able to advise you.

Even then, think carefully about how well the advice fits you and your situation. What we are cautioning you against is unasked-for advice. People will give you advice with the best of intentions. The trouble is that friends and family usually offer advice based only on their personal makeup and experience. Basically, each one says, "If I were in your situation, here's what I would do." The helpfulness and appropriateness of that advice will depend on how similar their makeup and experience are to yours. Sometimes there's a reasonable match, and their suggestion is helpful. Often there isn't much of a match and the suggestion that makes sense to them really doesn't fit you and your situation. It's not unusual for three friends to give you four conflicting pieces of advice—and a headache!

So have the courtesy to listen to those who offer you unasked-for advice, and the sense to consider if it is really helpful to you. It's your life and ultimately you make your own decisions.

> *So have the courtesy to listen to those who offer you unasked-for advice, and the sense to consider if it is really helpful to you.*

If someone wants to give you lots of unasked-for advice—we call such people "psychopests"—don't be afraid to assert yourself: "Thanks for your concern and suggestions. I appreciate the fact that you care. However, when you tell me what I should do, you are putting down my ability to run my life for myself, and that annoys me. I'd like you to wait for me to ask for your advice, when I feel I need it."

Helpful organizations

In addition to the help you should be willing to seek from individuals in your life, there are organizations you can get help from. These are even more important if you don't think you can count on any individuals. You may have no family living within reach and you may have been socially isolated, at least with no *close* friends, before your crisis began. Right now you may be telling yourself that you are all alone with your suffering and no one else cares. If you are, that would be both a symptom and a further cause of your depression. And it's just not true.

Most people have the capacity to be caring, when the opportunity is given to them. Some people express their care for others by joining helpful organizations. They will be glad to lend a hand if you invite them to. Your local women's group or religious institution, the Salvation Army or the Red Cross may be places to start. Many self-help groups offer support for people coping with particular kinds of crises, such as the National SIDS Alliance, Alzheimer's Association and so on. In times of personal despair, try calling one of many emergency telephone counseling services, *hotlines*, listed inside the front cover of the telephone book and in the Resources section of this book (see page 215). In fact, there are so many helping organizations that we can't possibly list them all.

Don't wallow in your post-crisis depression by telling yourself you're alone and no one understands or cares about you. Even if that's true right now, it's probably because you haven't given anyone the chance to understand and care. Maybe the first practical step you take to begin your recovery will be to contact a helpful organization, especially if you don't think you have any friends, family or associates you can lean on right now.

Drugs?

You may discover some helpful objects, such as a walking stick or wheelchair, in addition to helpful people and organizations. We don't discuss such objects in detail because they will probably be recommended by whoever is giving you treatment or counseling. We do caution you against talking yourself out of using them because they are "a sign of weakness." We have seen people unnecessarily increase the effect of a crisis and slow down and limit their recovery by refusing to use helpful

Life can be hard enough for crisis victims. Don't make it harder for yourself.

objects. If temporarily using an aid helps you recover, that sounds more like common sense than weakness. If one result of your crisis is that you have to use a helping object for the rest of your life, then coming to terms with that is an essential part of your recovery. Life can be hard enough for crisis victims. Don't make it harder for yourself.

A helpful object you are likely to be offered is a drug, prescribed or social. That's part of the Hollywood image of a crisis. The heroine is informed of the death of her husband, swoons to the floor and is immediately sedated up to the eyeballs by her kindly old doctor. Or the hero returns from a harrowing experience and proceeds to polish off a bottle of whiskey. However popular these ideas may be, they're usually a mistake. Now, don't get us wrong. You may think that because we are psychologists we are automatically against the use of drugs. That's not true. In fact, we have done our own research on the combined use of drugs and psychotherapy to manage some problems. What we are opposed to is the unwise or unnecessary use of drugs to suppress what are essentially normal reactions to a patient's life situation. For example, if someone is depressed because her marriage is not working, we think she is better off doing something to fix or get out of the marriage, rather than taking antidepressant drugs to put up with it.

We emphasize that the Crisis Response and Recovery Cycle are the normal reactions of someone who has experienced a crisis situation. You *should* feel strong emotions during and after a crisis. We also emphasize that the key to a successful recovery is to accept and work through those feelings, not deny them. Immediately using a strong drug to block your feelings is another way of denying them. You haven't avoided the feelings, only postponed them. Meanwhile the drug is probably reducing your ability to begin the practical aspects of coping, such as those we describe above. If you keep using the drug, you keep postponing the necessary process of accepting and working through your feelings.

Immediately using a strong drug to block your feelings is another way of denying them.

Again we emphasize we are not simply antidrug. If you are too upset to even begin to think straight, if the emotional pain after your crisis is too much to bear immediately, then you might benefit from *temporarily* postponing your recovery. Just make sure that it is temporary and that you don't fall into the trap of believing that drugs are an alternative to working through your recovery. They aren't. Sooner or later the normal stress reactions catch up with a crisis victim, often worsened because they were suppressed. You gain nothing from trying to postpone the emotional work of your recovery indefinitely.

The most common forms of drug dependence in our society are those involving social drugs, such as alcohol, and prescribed drugs, such as antianxiety and antidepressant drugs. If you ever start to think that your drug is *necessary* instead of helpful, meaning you start to believe you could not get by without it, you are getting a strong warning of developing drug dependence. If you can't ease yourself off the drug, it's time you got some professional help. Don't let your crisis leave you a junkie, no matter how "respectable" your drug of dependence is.

Depression, Guilt, Anger, Mood Swings, Sleep Problems

In chapter 1 we describe the common components of the recovery cycle: shock, depression, mood swings, anger, philosophical reflection and laying to rest. Some of them will most likely happen to every crisis victim, so we outline detailed approaches to managing each in later chapters. Because these are normal components of recovering from a crisis, you may need to do no more than realize they are normal, accept them as a temporary part of your life and gradually work through them. Even then you may find the suggestions in the relevant chapters helpful for just managing your normal stress reactions more easily. However, if you are not progressing through your recovery, if some part of it has grown out of proportion and is interfering with your return to normal functioning, then you owe it to yourself to tackle that obstacle by working carefully through the relevant chapter, or getting some professional help if self-help isn't working.

Given the normal variability of humans and our broad definition of a crisis, you could easily be having other strong emotions besides the ones just mentioned—*and that also would be normal*. The suggestions in chapter 8 should help you manage your strong emotions better.

In chapter 1 we describe some of the physical reactions to crisis (such as shock, fainting, nausea, loss of bladder and bowel control) and we emphasize their involuntary but normal nature. You may have physical reactions during the recovery cycle as well, such as loss of appetite, sleep disturbances and diarrhea. As with your emotional reactions, don't add to your burdens by overreacting to these normal physical reactions. We give you suggestions for sleeping better in chapter 11. If your diarrhea or loss of appetite doesn't fade as you get your life organized again and work through your recovery, see your doctor.

What Did It All Mean?

Many crisis victims, particularly victims of traumatic crises, spend a lot of time reviewing their experience, trying to make some sense of it. In truth, there may be nothing rational about it, which is hard for most of us to accept. Whether you review the meaning of your experience privately, in your head, or publicly, by some formal commission, you may discover some possible or definite factors that contributed to your crisis. As a result, you may do some things differently in the future and so reduce the probability of being a crisis victim again. That makes good sense to us.

But your review may turn up no identifiable causes, or none you can do anything about. As we describe in chapter 1, you will be faced with the inescapable facts of your personal vulnerability and mortality and the role that luck plays in your life. We are not denying that we all live in a cause-and-effect world. In principle, every crisis could be explained in terms of its causes. But in practice many of those causes are so obscure, or so remote in time or place, that there would be little or nothing we could do about them, even if we could discover them. So finally we have to say, "It was bad luck."

Some people accept this, and lay their crises to rest as bad memories not to be dwelt on any more than necessary. Many victims say they realize they have been changed forever by their crisis experience. Some discover religion. Some abandon religion. We can't tell you what your experience meant to you. We are not philosophers and we don't have a "Deep Thought" computer to tell us the meaning of life, death and crises. As psychologists we *do* want to point out to you that it's possible to accept the changes in yourself brought on by your crisis experience, to accept your personal vulnerability, mortality and the intrusion of luck into your life, and still get on with living it quite successfully.

8

How to Manage Your Emotional Reactions

A crisis is an event that causes you to experience unusually strong emotions, so strong they interfere with your normal functioning. The strength of the emotional reactions to a crisis makes them potential problems. Most of us are not prepared for dealing with strong emotions, in ourselves or in others. So we often make two mistakes when confronted with them: We may try to deny them, to pretend they're not there or not that strong, or we may get swamped by them and wind up exaggerating them unnecessarily. Neither of these common mistakes will help you cope with your crisis, so in this chapter we offer you more effective ways to manage your emotional reactions, whether during a prolonged crisis or during recovery after your crisis.

Feeling Better by Thinking Straighter

Mental relaxation is a procedure you can use to manage your feelings. We use that name to show that it is different from *muscular relaxation* (trying to relax your body physically) but similar in purpose because it is intended to help you feel more relaxed and comfortable. The difference between mental and muscular relaxation is that instead of just trying to relax your body, which many people do not find helpful or even possible, you use your mind to relax your emotions. As you will see, it is an active coping skill, even if the activity is taking place mostly inside your head. The purpose of mental relaxation in this book is to help you

Mental Relaxation: Feeling Better by Thinking Straighter

1. Whenever you feel bad, say a coping statement to yourself and back it up with constructive action.

2. Before or after peaks of feeling bad, teach yourself to think more rationally
   - by finding the common mistakes in how you are thinking
   - by finding the irrational beliefs in what you are thinking
   - by practicing a more rational viewpoint

cope with the strong emotional reactions you have as a result of your crisis. It is also a useful skill in many aspects of your life. It is the backbone of our approach to many problems, including stress management and improving troubled relationships. After you come to terms with your crisis and lay it to rest, we encourage you to see mental relaxation as a coping skill you can use to help you tackle any problem in your life that involves strong emotional reactions. The basic plan for mental relaxation is outlined in the box above.

The process of mental relaxation can seem hard at first. We have broken it down into several steps that we will explain one at a time. It also helps to learn mental relaxation as a written exercise, at least until you feel you've mastered it. So we have designed a form, called the "Mental Relaxation Report" because it reports your attempt to use mental relaxation. Two examples of this report are at the end of this chapter (pages 154–157) in addition to a blank form that you can copy for your own use. We use the examples as we work through our explanation of mental relaxation, so you will need to keep referring to it.

The coping statement

During and soon after your crisis, you may feel bad to some degree, most of the time. You are likely to experience peaks of feeling bad, times when your bad feelings become stronger. Later in your recovery, especially if you experience the common swings in mood, there will be times when you feel good, but then your bad feelings will return, sometimes with a vengeance. Long after you have laid your crisis to rest, life may suddenly remind you of it in some way and that will of course make you feel bad again. *At these times, when your bad feelings are peaking or returning, you can manage them better by saying a coping statement to yourself and backing it up with constructive action.*

The coping statement is a plan for coping with strong bad feelings. It is a set of instructions you give to yourself, whenever you feel bad. If you act on those instructions as you say them, your bad feelings should lessen. In our experience, people get their best results if they stick closely to our formula, so we encourage you to do the same. At first, we suggest you write out the coping statement and carry it around with you. The times you will need it most are when you feel worst and that's when it can be hard to think straight or remember something. If you have the coping statement written on a reminder card, you can pull it out and read it to yourself on the spot. Eventually you will memorize it.

It is important for you to create a statement that means something to you, so you are not just reciting it like a "magic formula." Let's take a look at creating an effective coping statement, one piece at a time.

The Basic Formula for a Coping Statement

I expect some bad feelings in this situation, but I'll cope;

I won't deny my feelings, but I also won't dwell on them;

if possible, I'll do something constructive to improve this situation now;

if not, I'll do something else, pleasant or constructive, to distract me.

"I expect some bad feelings in this situation, but I'll cope." We emphasize the need for you to accept the normality of your emotional reactions to a crisis (and the same applies to other trouble spots in your life). So you should begin coping by reminding yourself that it's normal to have bad feelings, under the circumstances. But then you should also remind yourself that you will cope with feeling bad. Some people have trouble accepting this, because they mistakenly think that *to cope* means *to stop feeling bad*, and they don't stop feeling bad. To have no bad feelings actually represents mastery of a situation. You might eventually achieve mastery of a past crisis, but that's not your goal right now. By *cope*, we mean *manage* or *get by*, and that's what you should mean when you tell yourself you "will cope": For example, "I expect to have some normal bad feelings under these circumstances, but I will manage them."

"I won't try to deny my feelings, but I also won't dwell on them." We have already pointed out that denial and dwelling are the two most common mistakes people make when faced with strong feelings and that they actually make you feel worse. Trying to deny feelings can involve saying, "This is silly. I shouldn't be feeling like this now" or "It's crazy (or weak or cowardly or stupid) to feel like this. What's wrong with me?" Denial boils down to telling yourself you should not feel bad about a crisis. In extreme cases, it involves not even admitting to yourself how bad you are feeling. We think trying to deny your feelings really is crazy, because normal people have bad feelings in response to crises. If you fall into this trap, you are likely to end up feeling bad about feeling bad, because you have told yourself that you shouldn't be feeling bad.

> *If you fall into this trap, you are likely to end up feeling bad about feeling bad, because you have told yourself that you shouldn't be feeling bad.*

That sounds silly, but look around you at how often people do it. "What's wrong with me? Why am I getting upset?" And they get upset about getting upset, or angry about being angry, or depressed about being depressed. Trying to deny your bad feelings only makes them worse. To help yourself cope better, now tell yourself *not* to try to deny your feelings.

The other common mistake when confronted by strong bad feelings is to wallow in them. You fall into this mistake if you dwell on your bad feelings, stewing over your crisis. After an hour of good solid stewing you will usually feel worse, and you'll have achieved nothing else. It hasn't taken away your crisis. It hasn't made it any more or less likely that you may have another crisis some time in your life. The only real effect of dwelling on your bad feelings and stewing over your crisis will be *to make you feel worse.*

Some review of a crisis is a normal part of recovery as you try to come to terms with your experience, why it happened to you and what it means. We are not discouraging you from this normal reaction. It may be hard at times, but we suggest you try to discriminate between this normal review and self-defeating stewing. Your most reliable guide will be your feelings. If reviewing your experience is helping you work through your recovery, then you should gradually review less and less and your bad feelings should also lessen, as you arrive at some acceptance. If you are just stewing, you won't mull over the experience any less and your bad feelings won't lessen. In fact, they may get worse, especially anger or depression. Then it is time for you to tell yourself to stop dwelling unnecessarily on your bad feelings and your crisis. Of course, it's easier to tell yourself something than it is to do it. Then it's time for the next part of your coping statement.

"If possible, I'll do something constructive to improve the situation now." The best way to stop yourself from dwelling unnecessarily on your bad feelings is to get yourself in gear and do something practical, preferably something to improve your situation directly. Constructive action is the best cure for morbid dwelling. If you are coping with an ongoing crisis, there may be something

> *Constructive action is the best cure for morbid dwelling.*

you can do about it right now. Then plan what you can do, give yourself a shove and do it! If you need help, get it.

If the crisis is now over, you are probably trying to cope with the strong feelings that occur during recovery. The crisis itself is past, so there is nothing practical you can do about that, although this can be hard to accept. You *can* do something practical about your feelings, and that is to share them constructively. We explain how to do that in the next chapter. But for the original cause of your bad feelings, your crisis experience, there may be nothing you can do about it, at least not now. During an ongoing, prolonged crisis, there will still be many times when you can do nothing practical about the crisis. You can't work on it all of the time. Maybe you can do something tomorrow, or next week, but you can't do anything now, apart from trying to share your feelings constructively with anyone who may be affected by them. So it's time for the distraction strategy.

"If not, I'll do something else, pleasant or constructive, to distract me." There is simply no value in dwelling unnecessarily on something you can't change, like your crisis. But there may be no action you can take to directly affect your crisis and keep you from dwelling on it. If that's the case, and it often is for people working through recovery, you need some other activity to block that unnecessary dwelling. In other words, you need a distraction. You can distract yourself with any activity that will occupy your mind. It could be a constructive, purposeful activity, like getting on with a job or working on a hobby project, or it could be a pleasant activity, such as reading a book, watching a movie, socializing with a friend or some other way of having fun. What matters is that it occupies your mind so that you aren't tempted to slip back into stewing over a situation you can do nothing about.

Again, we are talking about aiming for a balance between accepting the normal crisis reactions and working through them to recovery, without trying to either deny or exaggerate them. If you bury yourself so completely in distracting activities that you never have the chance to experience even the normal crisis reactions, that becomes denial and your emotions will probably catch up with you later. A common example is the person who loses a close relationship through separation and immediately rushes into a wild social life, dating anything that moves. Sooner or later the postponed grief and anger catch up, usually magnified by the attempt at denial. You will not fall into this trap if you follow the coping statement as we have outlined it, because you will first tell yourself to expect the normal bad feelings that come from a crisis and *then* find a distracting activity to prevent dwelling on your feelings, not to deny them altogether.

If you often need to use this distraction strategy, and many people do during the recovery cycle, it pays to do some planning *before* you need it. If you wait until you are feeling about as low as you can go, then decide you need a distracting activity, you are not in the best frame of mind to find one. Use some of the time when you are not feeling so bad to prepare a couple of possible distractions for the rougher times. Get an appealing book or video, start a project, line up a friend to visit. Have one or two possible distracting activities ready to go so that the next time you feel unbearably bad, it won't take much effort to get into one.

Use some of the time when you are not feeling so bad to prepare a couple of possible distractions for the rougher times.

Many people have a hard time doing something that needs to be done—a part of their work or a regular chore that does not occupy their minds. It's too simple, too habitual, too routine to need much thought. But it needs to be done and you can't easily postpone it until you're in a better frame of mind. So you work your way through this activity mechanically while your unoccupied mind stews things over, building up your bad feelings. In this case, you need to find a distracting activity that won't prevent you from completing the necessary tasks but will occupy your spare mental space to keep you from stewing. Find something to listen to, a radio program (or even a television program, if the visual distraction won't interfere too much) or an audiocassette. In addition to music, books on tape are becoming so popular, you can find them in stores that rent videos, the library, audiobook clubs or even in stores that rent audiobooks exclusively.

Mental Relaxation: Step by Step

To help you master mental relaxation, we will work through two examples, one step at a time, as we introduce the steps to you. The following situations correspond to the sample "Mental Relaxation Report Form" on pages 154 and 156, so take a look at them now.

Example one

The first is the case of a young bank teller who was the victim of an armed robbery. The actual robbery only lasted a few minutes, during which the robber pointed a gun at the teller, threatening to "blow his head off!" if he did not hand over all the money in his reach. The teller did as he was told and the robber escaped and has not been caught. The teller has returned to work but becomes frightened whenever he has to serve a customer who looks like the robber, and he is then likely to feel depressed for several days afterward. To begin mental relaxation, he writes on the report form a brief description of the situation that now causes his burst of bad feelings and a statement of his feelings. Check these for yourself on page 154.

Practical Exercise

We suggest you start learning how to use mental relaxation right now, by starting your own report. On the blank report form on page 158 (or a copy of it), write a brief description of a situation that involves strong bad feelings for you and list the feelings, as we have done in our examples. A common problem people have at this step is not being able to pinpoint any particular situation that triggered the increased or returned bad feelings. In our two examples, the situations that triggered the strong bad feelings are pretty obvious, but that isn't always the case. If there is no apparent trigger for your bad feelings in your immediate situation, you will usually find that it was something inside you, such as thinking about your crisis or dwelling on your bad feelings. In that case, that's what you record on your report form: for example, "Thinking about how horrible my experience was."

Example two
The second example involves a mother whose daughter has been diagnosed with a life-threatening illness. She visits her daughter in a children's hospital regularly, trying to give her support because the illness and its treatment are debilitating for the child, who knows it is possible she may die. The mother is severely depressed and sometimes angry after each visit to her daughter. She begins mental relaxation by recording the situation and her feelings on the report form. You can see these in the second example, on page 156.

Say the coping statement to yourself
After you recognize your strong bad feelings and identify the apparent trigger, whether it was something outside or inside you, you begin mental relaxation by saying the coping statement to yourself. Take a look at the examples on pages 154 and 156.

Practical Exercise

Create and say your own coping statement by fitting the standard formula to your feelings and trigger. Even if you never use any of the other steps in mental relaxation, consistent use of the coping statement will help you to accept and work through your bad feelings. Can you start using it right now in other situations?

And back it up with constructive action
Saying the coping statement is the first important step you can take to manage your bad feelings better, but you also need to act on the statement. Your coping statement tells you to do something constructive, either to improve the situation or, if that's not possible, to distract yourself. If you aren't sure what to do, ask for suggestions from relatives, friends, associates or a professional counselor. Identify and use your resources.

Example one
Our young bank teller checks that all reasonable safety precautions are taken at work, and then reminds himself to use the calming response (described later in this chapter) to cope with his feelings

of fear at work. If he still feels depressed later, he again uses the coping statement and then uses his distracting activities to prevent any unnecessary stewing and to lift his mood (see chapter 10).

Example two

The mother with the seriously ill child reminds herself that she has taken all possible practical steps to deal with her daughter's illness and she can do nothing else to tackle the crisis itself. She then reminds herself that she can help her daughter most if she takes care of her own feelings, too, so she shares them constructively with her husband (see the next chapter) and then tries to lift her mood a little with some distracting activity (see chapter 10).

These practical steps are written in our two examples on pages 154 and 156.

Practical Exercise

What practical steps can you figure out to help yourself cope? If you are coping with an ongoing crisis, is there anything you can do now to tackle it directly? Otherwise, what distracting activities can you use to prevent any unnecessary stewing about it? If you are stuck for ideas, can you get some help? Whom will you ask? You do have a choice now, either to sit still and let yourself be overwhelmed by bad feelings or get moving and do something constructive. We recommend action.

Teach yourself to think rationally

Saying a coping statement and backing it up with constructive action are what you can do at the actual time of strong bad feelings. As we said, that part of the mental relaxation procedure should be helpful on its own, even if you never try anything else. But you can manage your bad feelings even better if you are willing to do a little work in between your periods of feeling bad. The goal of this work is to help you think about your crisis as rationally as possible so that it doesn't affect you any more than it has to. You can do this work after your present struggle with strong feelings has subsided. Or, if you can predict situations that are likely to trigger strong bad feelings, you can do this work beforehand and prepare yourself mentally to cope better with those situations when they occur. As the box on page 145 shows, you can prepare by noticing your thoughts about the situation, then testing those thoughts for mistakes and irrationality. Then you'll be able to work out a more realistic way of thinking about the situation.

What was your original self-talk?

By "your original self-talk" we mean what is going through your mind at the time you are actually having the strong bad feelings. Self-talk can be in words—you are thinking something—or images—you are imagining something. Humans actually do a lot of their thinking in images, either imagining again some past experience (like a crisis) or imagining how things might turn out in the future.

Mental relaxation is based on the scientific theory that your self-talk has a major influence over your feelings, especially how strong and how persistent they are. According to this theory, strong and long-lasting bad feelings are the result of mistakes in your self-talk. To get rid of the exaggeration in your feelings, you must find these mistakes. First, you need to work out what your self-talk is when you are in the trigger situation.

> *strong and long-lasting bad feelings are the result of mistakes in your self-talk.*

Example one

When the bank teller considers his self-talk, he finds that when he is frightened at work he is thinking, "This is the same guy. It's another robbery. It's going to happen again!" When he is depressed later, he is thinking, "I'm always going to be haunted by what happened to me. I'll never feel okay at work again."

Example two

The mother of the ill child finds she is imagining her little girl dying. Then she thinks angrily, "Why can't they do something to help her?" See their self-talk recorded in the examples on pages 155 and 156.

Practical Exercise

Now figure out your own self-talk. This is sometimes difficult, at first. Your self-talk may be hard to remember. The best approach is to try to imagine yourself in the trigger situation as vividly as you can. Then imagine how you feel in that situation. Now try to figure out what you would be thinking or imagining while you are experiencing those feelings. If you still can't guess, leave it until the next time you are in the trigger situation, then pay attention to your self-talk. You may be surprised just how much there is! Whenever you can figure out your original self-talk, record it in the next space of your report form on page 158.

   If you can't figure it out now, wait until the next time you experience strong bad feelings. Meanwhile, you can skip over the next step and go on to the one after.

Test your self-talk for mistakes

The problem for us humans is that we tend to believe our own thoughts. At least at the time we say something to ourselves, we accept it as accurate and realistic. Often it isn't. We often make mistakes in how we think about or imagine things. When you accept mistakes in your self-talk as accurate, those mistakes will make extra bad feelings for you. The situation will quite normally make you feel bad anyway, but your thinking mistakes are unnecessarily adding to those feelings. To get rid of the extra bad feelings, you must identify and get rid of the mistakes. To help you do this, we have listed the six common thinking mistakes on page 145. These were originally identified by psychiatrist Dr. Aaron Beck as a major cause of depression, but we have found they can contribute to any strong bad feeling. Take a look at them now.

> *The problem for us humans is that we tend to believe our own thoughts.*

Common Mistakes in Thinking

1. Overgeneralizing

This involves drawing a general conclusion on the basis of only one incident. You are telling yourself that, if something was true in one case, it will apply to any case that is remotely similar. In fact, life is rarely that simple.

2. Black-and-white thinking

This means seeing things as only one extreme or the other, such as telling yourself a friendship must be fantastic or else it's horrible. In the real world, there are many shades of gray.

3. "Who needs evidence?"

This mistake involves drawing a conclusion without any real evidence to support it, or even in spite of contradictory evidence! For example, saying no one likes you when you do have some friends and could not possibly have asked *everybody*. Ask yourself, "What is the real world evidence to support my conclusions in this self-talk?"

4. Looking at the world through deep-blue glasses

This means focusing on what is wrong and blowing it out of proportion—your mistakes, your failures, your problems—and ignoring or belittling anything that's right—your successes, good times and good fortune. Looking at the world through rose-colored glasses can be misleading, too. Avoid distorting the world in either direction.

5. Imagining the worst

This is a special case of exaggeration, or looking at the world through deep-blue glasses, but it is so common that it deserves a mention of its own: Imagining the worst means assuming the worst possible outcome for any event, usually so exaggerated that it's really improbable, if not impossible.

6. Taking things personally

This means blaming yourself for everything wrong, even when you are only partly or not at all responsible: for example, blaming only yourself for problems in your marriage (we'll bet your spouse contributes to them, too). If you really run the whole universe, please tell us how. Taking things personally can also mean assuming that everybody notices every mistake you make, that you are the center of everybody's (disapproving) attention. You will usually discover that most people are too busy worrying about their own problems to even notice yours.

Example one

When the bank teller reads through the list of thinking mistakes and looks at the self-talk he has recorded, he decides he is slipping into thinking mistakes number one ("Everyone who looks like the bank robber is going to be one"), number three (he has no real evidence that this customer is even likely to be a robber) and number five (he expects to be robbed again and never to get over his crisis experience).

Example two

When the mother tests her self-talk, she decides she was making thinking mistakes number two (telling herself that because her daughter hasn't completely recovered, nothing helpful is being done for her) and number five (imagining her daughter dying when that won't necessarily happen).

Each recorded the thinking mistakes they have identified in the examples on pages 155 and 157.

Practical Exercise

At this step, read through the descriptions of the thinking mistakes and try to identify which have crept into the self-talk you recorded on your report form. You are focusing now on the situation you describe on your report form. Most of us make all of the common thinking mistakes at some time, but that's not the point of the exercise. Which common thinking mistakes can you find in the self-talk you have just written down? Sometimes it's obvious and easy; sometimes it isn't. People who are feeling depressed or angry are sometimes reluctant to admit that there might be any mistakes in their view of the world: "It really is like that, and that's why I feel so bad." For your own sake, to save yourself from unnecessary bad feelings, take a critical look at your self-talk.

Remember you are doing this exercise for your own good, so don't be afraid to find out that you make occasional mistakes (like the rest of us).

Look for the underlying irrational beliefs

Humans are not born able to think. Our brains do a lot of growing after birth, so thinking only begins to develop after birth and, in fact, develops throughout childhood and adolescence. We learn how and what to think from the examples of our family and friends, from school and other cultural influences, such as the media. The problem is, most of what we usually learn about thinking is irrational or unrealistic. Below we have listed ten popular irrational beliefs, ten attitudes that most of us were exposed to as we grew up. As a result, most of us are influenced by these beliefs at different times. The problem with that, of course, is that *they are irrational.* When you allow them to influence you, you are likely to feel and handle life worse than is necessary. These beliefs were originally described by psychologist Dr. Albert Ellis, who saw them as the cause of all psychological problems. We have rewritten them in plainer English. Take a look at them now.

Ten Popular Irrational Beliefs

1. I must be loved, or at least liked, and approved of by every significant person I meet.

2. To be worthwhile, I must be completely competent, make no mistakes and achieve in every possible way.

3. Some people are bad or wicked, and they should be blamed and punished for this.

4. It is terrible, nearly the end of the world, when things aren't the way I would like them to be.

5. Human unhappiness, including mine, is caused by factors outside my control, so I can't do much about it.

6. If something might be dangerous, unpleasant or frightening, I should worry about it a lot.

7. It's easier to put off something difficult or unpleasant than it is to face up to it.

8. I need someone stronger than myself to depend on.

9. My problems were caused by events in my past—that's why I have my problems now.

10. I should be very upset by other people's problems.

Example one

After reading through the list of irrational beliefs, the bank teller decides his reaction at work is influenced by irrational beliefs number six (worrying about another bank robbery before it has even happened, and worrying about never getting over his experience before he has had time to) and number nine (telling himself that his present distress is due entirely to his past robbery experience).

Example two

The mother decides her reaction has been influenced by irrational beliefs number six (dwelling on the possibility of her daughter dying before it has happened) and number five (seeing herself as totally helpless in the situation).

They have each recorded the irrational beliefs identified in their examples on pages 155 and 157.

Practical Exercise

At this step, read through the list of popular irrational beliefs to decide which were influencing your reaction to your trigger situation. Notice you are *not* asking yourself, "Which of these do I completely and wholeheartedly believe?" Written out in black and white, the irrational beliefs are obviously exaggerated and unrealistic. You are looking for *influence*, not total acceptance. The question is, "Which of these did I allow to influence my reaction in that situation, even if I recognize it as irrational when I read it?"

Read the irrational beliefs one at a time, pausing at each one to decide whether it has influenced you on this occasion. Notice that you are again focusing on just this trigger situation. Most people have been influenced by many of the irrational beliefs at some time, but that's not the question now. Again, remember that this exercise is strictly for your own benefit, so don't be afraid to admit that sometimes you are a little irrational (like the rest of us). Record the irrational belief(s) that you identify on your report form.

We are suggesting you test your self-talk for *both* thinking mistakes and irrational beliefs because researchers have found that the more you challenge your old self-talk, the more effective mental relaxation is. The thinking mistakes are errors in *how* you are thinking; the irrational beliefs are errors in *what* you are thinking. So we are encouraging you to question your original self-talk for both *style* and *content*.

Now practice a more rational view

By now you have identified common thinking mistakes you were making and underlying irrational beliefs that influenced you to overreact to your trigger situation. You have showed yourself that you have been unnecessarily increasing your natural bad feelings with mistaken and irrational self-talk. So now the question becomes, "What do I say to myself instead? If what I have been thinking or imagining in that trigger situation is mistaken and irrational, what do I say to myself instead, so I don't feel any worse than I have to?"

To help you plan better self-talk to use in that trigger situation in the future, we have listed ten rational ideas on page 150. These ideas should replace your irrational beliefs and help you avoid common thinking mistakes. Take a look at them now.

Example one

The bank teller reads over rational ideas number six and number nine. He applies number six to his own situation at work like this: "Worrying about the possibility of another robbery won't stop it from happening, it just makes me scared now. I have taken constructive steps to prepare for that possibility (making reasonable security arrangements) and that's as much as anyone can do. So I won't dwell on the future now." At home, he applies rational idea number six like this: "Worrying about never getting over my experience won't stop that from happening, it only makes it harder for me to cope. I have taken constructive steps to make sure I do get over it (starting a self-help program, getting appropriate counseling), and that's as much as anyone can do.

Ten Rational Ideas

1. I want to be loved, or liked, and approved of by *some* of the people in my life. I will feel disappointed or lonely when that doesn't happen, but I can cope with those feelings, and I can take constructive steps to make and keep better relationships.

2. I want to do some things well, most of the time. Like everybody, I will occasionally fail or make a mistake. Then I will feel bad, but I can cope with that, and I can take constructive steps to do better next time.

3. It is sad that most of us do some bad things from time to time, and some people do a lot of bad things. But making myself upset won't change that.

4. I am disappointed when things aren't the way I want them to be, but I can cope with that. Usually I can take constructive steps to make things more as I would like them to be, but if I can't, it doesn't help me to exaggerate my disappointment.

5. My problems may be influenced by factors outside my control, but my thoughts and actions also influence my problems, and they *are* under my control.

6. Worrying about something that might go wrong won't stop it from happening, it just makes me unhappy now! I can take constructive steps to prepare for possible problems, and that's as much as anyone can do. So I won't dwell on the future now.

7. Facing difficult situations will make me feel bad at the time, but I can cope with that. Putting off problems doesn't make them any easier, it just gives me more time to worry about them.

8. Support from others when I want it is great, but the only person I really need to rely on is myself.

9. My problems may have started because of past events, but what keeps them going now are my thoughts and actions, and they are under my control.

10. It is sad to see other people in trouble, but I don't help them by making myself miserable. I can cope with feeling sad, and sometimes I can take constructive steps to help them.

So I won't dwell on that possibility now." He applies rational idea number nine like this: "My fear at work and my depression at home certainly started with my robbery experience, but my thoughts and actions make those feelings stronger or longer-lasting than they have to be now, and my thoughts and actions are under my control. I can use mental relaxation to straighten my thoughts and I have planned some constructive actions." (See his report form for details of his planned actions.)

Example two

The mother applies rational idea number six like this: "Dwelling on the possibility of my daughter dying won't stop that from happening. It only makes me upset now and lessens the support I can give her. I have found good medical care for her, and that's as much as anyone can do. So I won't dwell on the future now." She applies rational idea number five like this: "My daughter's illness is influenced by factors outside my control, but my thoughts and actions about her illness *are* under my control and they will also influence how I feel and how much support I can give her. I can use mental relaxation to straighten my thoughts and I have planned some constructive actions. If my daughter does die, if I have done some clear thinking and constructive action, I will know that I did my best to help her." (See her report form for details of her planned actions.)

Practical Exercise

The numbers of the rational ideas in the box on page 150 match the numbers of the irrational beliefs in the box on page 147. Spend a few minutes reading the rational ideas that match the irrational beliefs you have picked as influencing your reactions. Try to figure out how you can apply each matching rational idea to your own particular trigger situation. Then try to think like that the next time the trigger situation occurs. It might help to write your rational ideas on reminder cards to carry with you.

By now you should have worked through one complete example of mental relaxation. If you haven't, we encourage you to stop reading to do one now. This is a practical self-help program and you will only benefit from it if you try the exercises instead of just reading about them. When you have tried one example for yourself, try a couple more while it's fresh in your mind. Most people master the procedure more easily if they do it in writing the first few times. After you've tried mental relaxation a couple times, you will probably see that it's not as hard to do as it looks. The hardest part of mental relaxation for most people is the need to do it over and over again. You are often trying to change some deep-seated thinking habits, and that takes persistence. So from now on, whenever you feel bad, not just because of your crisis experience but for any reason, use mental relaxation to help yourself feel better and to prompt yourself to do something constructive. Mental relaxation is a useful coping skill, long after you have laid your crisis to rest. Right now, make sure you can at least use the coping statement before you go to the next chapter.

Do You Need a Calming Response?

One of the practical steps the bank teller planned to take was to learn and use the calming response. You might find this helpful, too. The *calming response* is a quick coping skill, based on the quieting response developed for stress management by Dr. Charles Stroebel and his colleagues. The calming response is helpful for people whose strong feelings rise up quickly. The two most common strong feelings in crisis victims are panic and anger. The calming response is detailed in the box below.

The Calming Response

Step 1: Mentally detach from the situation and smile to yourself.

Step 2: Think, "Clear head, calm body."

Step 3: Take in one slow, deep breath.

Step 4: As you breathe out, relax your body, from head to toes.

The calming response is most effective if you use it right away, before your emotions are fully aroused. So the first trick is to learn your own early warning signals. What do you notice in your situation and in yourself that warns you that you are about to have a panic attack or become angry? Become sensitive to those early warning signals and use them to prompt you to begin a calming response. The whole response takes only six seconds, so you can do it on the spot without interfering with your activities. Other people will only notice that you are being thoughtful for a moment, which won't hurt your image.

Step 1: Mentally detach from the situation and smile to yourself. As soon as you step back from the situation, even mentally, it has less effect on you. Smiling to yourself helps you detach and adds the calming effect of humor. Just make sure you are smiling to yourself and not grinning at everybody else.

Step 2: Think, "Clear head, calm body." You are telling yourself that your mind will stay alert while you deal with the situation, but your body is about to relax.

Step 3: Take in one slow, deep breath. Your mind reacts to your body's reactions. Fast, shallow or irregular breathing makes you feel agitated. Taking control of your breathing helps you feel in control of your reaction.

Step 4: As you breathe out, relax your body, from head to toes. Imagine a wave of relaxation, starting in your head and flowing down through your body to your feet. Let the tension melt out of your body, like butter in the sun.

The calming response is a practical skill, so you will get better at it with regular practice. Try to find a couple of minutes each day; many short practice sessions work better than occasional long ones. Imagine yourself in a trigger situation that would likely make you panicky or angry, taking time to make it realistic in your mind. Then imagine yourself using the calming response, one step at a time, and restoring your self-control. This practice in your imagination will transfer well to the real world, especially if you use your early warning signals to prompt yourself to use the calming response *before* you get too upset.

Mental Relaxation Report Form
(example one)

Describe the situation that has triggered your bad feelings:

Being reminded of my robbery experience

Describe your feelings:

Frightened, then depressed

Say the coping statement to yourself (using your feelings and situation in the statement, if you like):

"I expect to feel frightened and then depressed when reminded of the robbery, but I'll cope; I won't deny my feelings, but I also won't dwell on them; if possible, I'll do something constructive to improve the situation now; if not, I'll do something else, pleasant or constructive, to distract me."

What constructive steps did you take or have you planned?

Take reasonable security precautions; use the calming response; lessen my depression with a coping statement and some distracting activities

What is your original self-talk in the situation?

> *This is another robbery. It's going to happen*
> *again. (Later:) I'm always going to be*
> *haunted by what happened. I'll never feel*
> *okay at work again.*

Which common thinking mistakes can you find in your self-talk? (List the number(s) from the box on page 145): *1, 3, 5*

Which irrational belief(s) influenced your original reaction? (List the number(s) from the box on page 147) *6, 9*

How can you apply the matching rational idea(s) (from the box on page 150) to your situation?

> *Worrying about the possibility of another robbery won't stop it*
> *from happening, it just makes me scared now. I have taken*
> *constructive steps to prepare for that possibility (making*
> *reasonable security arrangements) and that's as much as*
> *anyone can do. So I won't dwell on the future now.*
> *Worrying about never getting over my experience won't*
> *stop that from happening, it only makes it harder for me to*
> *cope. I have taken constructive steps to make sure I do get over*
> *it (starting a self-help program, getting appropriate*
> *counseling), and that's as much as anyone can do. So I won't*
> *dwell on that possibility now.*
> *My fear at work and my depression at home certainly*
> *started with my robbery experience, but my thoughts and*
> *actions make those feelings stronger or longer-lasting than*
> *they have to be now, and my thoughts and actions are under*
> *my control. I can use mental relaxation to straighten my*
> *thoughts and I have planned some constructive actions.*

Mental Relaxation Report Form
(example two)

Describe the situation that has triggered your bad feelings:

Visiting my daughter in the hospital

Describe your feelings:

Depressed, sometimes angry

Say the coping statement to yourself (using your feelings and situation in the statement, if you like):

"I expect to feel depressed and angry after I visit my daughter, but I'll cope; I won't deny my feelings, but I also won't dwell on them; if possible, I'll do something constructive to improve the situation now; if not, I'll do something else, pleasant or constructive, to distract me."

What constructive steps did you take or have you planned?

I have already arranged for good medical care; now, share my feelings with my husband, try to distract myself

What is your original self-talk in the situation?

Imagining my daughter dying. Thinking, "Why can't they do something to help her?"

Which common thinking mistakes can you find in your self-talk? (List the number(s) from the box on page 145): _____ 5, 2 _____

Which irrational belief(s) influenced your original reaction? (List the number(s) from the box on page 147) _____ 6, 5 _____

How can you apply the matching rational idea(s) (from the box on page 150) to your situation?

Dwelling on the possibility of my daughter dying won't stop that from happening. It only makes me upset now and lessens the support I can give her. I have found good medical care for her, and that's as much as anyone can do. So I won't dwell on the future now.

My daughter's illness is influenced by factors outside my control, but my thoughts and actions about her illness are under my control and they will also influence how I feel and how much support I can give her. I can use mental relaxation to straighten my thoughts and I have planned some constructive actions. If my daughter does die, if I have done some clear thinking and constructive action, I will know that I did my best to help her.

Mental Relaxation Report Form

Describe the situation that has triggered your bad feelings:

_____

_____

_____

Describe your feelings:

_____

_____

_____

Say the coping statement to yourself (using your feelings and situation in the statement, if you like):

"I expect some bad feelings in this situation, but I'll cope; I won't deny my feelings, but I also won't dwell on them; if possible, I'll do something constructive to improve the situation now; if not, I'll do something else, pleasant or constructive, to distract me."

What constructive steps did you take or have you planned?

_____

_____

_____

_____

_____

What is your original self-talk in the situation?

_____

_____

_____

Which common thinking mistakes can you find in your self-talk? (List the number(s) from the box on page 145): _____

Which irrational belief(s) influenced your original reaction? (List the number(s) from the box on page 147) _____

How can you apply the matching rational idea(s) (from the box on page 150) to your situation?

_____

_____

_____

_____

_____

_____

_____

_____

_____

_____

_____

_____

_____

_____

_____

_____

_____

_____

_____

_____

_____

_____

_____

9

How to Share Your Feelings Constructively

The defining characteristic of a crisis is the unusually strong emotions it causes in you, at the time and afterward. We devote the previous chapter to suggestions for managing those emotions constructively so you can accept their normality, without letting them be any stronger or last any longer than they have to. The next step in our basic plan for coping with a crisis is to share those strong emotions constructively. This should protect you from the risk of bottling up your feelings, protect your important relationships from unnecessary strain and allow you to get the important emotional support available from family and friends. Communication is a two-way process: Share this chapter (if not the entire book) with other important people in your life.

We humans don't really have a choice about sharing our emotions. Depending on the circumstances, from 60 to 93 percent of your emotional impact on someone else is nonverbal. You convey your emotions not so much by what you say as by how you say it (or don't say it). You express your feelings through your body language and facial expression.

> *You convey your emotions not so much by what you say as by how you say it (or don't say it).*

Some people, like actors, diplomats and salespeople, may be trained to hide or fake those nonverbal messages, and sociopaths seem to have a knack for this, too. Unless you belong to one of these groups, you should accept that you will unavoidably share most of your feelings nonverbally, regardless of what you do or don't say. Your real choice is not "Will I share my feelings?" but "How will I share my feelings?"

If your nonverbal message to others is that you obviously feel bad, but you say nothing about it, then you are actually sending them two messages: first, that you feel bad, but second, that you don't want to talk about it. That makes the people around you guess how you feel and why, and what they guess is usually worse than anything you would have said. The big risk is that they will guess you feel bad about *them* when really your bad feelings are the result of your crisis experience. Without clear communication from you to correct their mistaken guess, your bad feelings will put a strain on those relationships.

If your nonverbal message to others is that you obviously feel bad, but you deny it—saying, "I'm okay" when everything about you says you're not—then again you are sending two contradictory messages. This time it's even harder for other people because, in addition to making them guess about the true nature and cause of your feelings, you are forcing them to argue with you if *they* want to discuss your feelings. Again, you are putting an unnecessary strain on that relationship. You can avoid the risks of bottling up your feelings and straining important relationships by telling people how you feel, clearly and constructively. We call this *leveling*.

Leveling

If you are a crisis victim, you will usually be the person with strong feelings, which means you'll usually be the one leveling with others. Those around you will usually be the ones listening and understanding, skills we describe in detail later in this chapter. But your crisis and your reactions can understandably trigger some strong feelings in those around you, so they may also need to level sometimes while *you* listen and understand. They shouldn't bottle up or deny their feelings to you for exactly the same reasons you shouldn't.

They shouldn't bottle up or deny their feelings to you for exactly the same reasons you shouldn't.

Whenever you or someone involved with you has strong feelings, then you or she should level about them.

You can level about your feelings under two general circumstances, depending on what the trigger was for your feelings. If the trigger was not the behavior of the person you are talking to—for example, the trigger was your crisis experience—then you level by simply announcing your feelings and the trigger. For example, "I've been remembering what happened to me and now I feel depressed." If the trigger was the behavior of the person you are talking to—something he has done has triggered your feelings—then you level with an *X-Y-Z statement*: "When you did X, the effect on me was Y and I felt Z." We explain X-Y-Z statements in more detail starting on page 164.

While you are coping with your crisis, the crisis itself will usually be the major cause of your strong feelings, not the behavior of the person you are talking to. We focus on that kind of leveling first. During or soon after a crisis experience, the crisis itself will be the direct trigger of your feelings. For example, a holdup victim might say, "I feel really sick and frightened now that it's over." Or the parent of a dying child might come home from a hospital visit and say, "She was looking really sick today and I'm just miserable."

Later in the recovery cycle your crisis experience will be an indirect trigger of your present feelings, which have actually been triggered by some present reminder. For example, several months after separation, a woman might say, "I saw a man today who looked just like my husband and that made me really sad again." Or a man who was injured by a drunk driver might say, "I've been thinking about that rat who ran into me and how lightly he got off, and now I'm feeling angry again."

Sometimes during the recovery cycle you may not be able to identify an immediate trigger for your feelings. You know you feel terrible, but you can't remember anything that might have triggered it. This sometimes discourages people from sharing their feelings. They think the emotions are not "justified" because there is no apparent cause. It is just as important that you level then, too.

> ## Practical Exercise
>
> Pause for a few minutes and figure out some leveling statements you could use to share strong feelings with important people in your life when they are not the trigger for those feelings. Look at the examples above and follow the basic formula: "Because of this trigger, I am now feeling this way" or "I don't know what's caused it, but now I am feeling like this."
>
> Practice your leveling statements in your imagination. Look for chances to use them.

You simply report that you can't identify the trigger. For example, "I don't know why, but today I'm feeling really angry." Then you save others from guessing that you are angry with them when that isn't the case.

The X-Y-Z formula

The other situation in which you level is when the trigger for your bad feelings is the behavior of the person you are talking to. The most constructive way to tell someone how you feel about his behavior is to use the X-Y-Z formula: "When you did X, the effect on me was Y and I felt Z."

For example, "When you tell me to forget about what happened to me, it stops me from telling you how I really feel, and I feel even worse." Or, "When you tell me I should have stayed home that day, you're blaming me for something that wasn't my fault and that makes me angry."

Leveling with the X-Y-Z formula tells the other person exactly what she did, how it has affected you and how you feel about it. It is the most effective way to share any strong feelings within any relationship. At first, figuring out the right statement takes some thought, and it will feel artificial and awkward. But with some practice, it becomes your natural way of sharing important feelings. So let's go over the formula one part at a time.

When you do "X"

This should be a simple description of the other person's behavior, a report of what he actually said or did. For example, you might begin a leveling statement with "When you drive at eighty in heavy traffic . . ." With this beginning, the other person knows exactly which part of his behavior has upset you.

Don't make vague statements. For example, "When you do things that remind me of my accident . . ." The other person has to guess what he has done that has reminded you of your accident.

Don't level with interpretations. For example, "When you don't care how I feel . . ." The other person has to guess which part of her behavior seems uncaring to you. Your interpretations of other people's behavior are your own thoughts and therefore your own responsibility. If you are constantly thinking negative thoughts about the people around you, it's time you tested the reality of your thinking, using the steps in the last chapter.

> *Your interpretations of other people's behavior are your own thoughts and therefore your own responsibility.*

Don't overgeneralize. For example, "When you *always* drive fast . . ." or "When you *never* drive slowly . . ." Overgeneralizations are rarely true and they invite the other person to look for the exception: "Well, I drove slowly last week." This avoids your concern that he is driving quickly now.

Don't assassinate her character. For example, "You are a thoughtless and uncaring person." Again, she has to guess what she has done to give you that impression and she will probably be defensive about such a harsh accusation. A big advantage to our formula is that it gets you to focus on the other person's *behavior*, not her character. She can always change her behavior.

The effect on me is "Y"

This should be a brief, clear description of how the other person's behavior has *directly* affected you. If you tell people how you have been directly affected by their behavior, they pay more attention to your leveling and they may be more willing to change their behavior. Continuing our example, your leveling statement now becomes, "When you drive at eighty in heavy traffic, it reminds me of my accident . . ." Now the other person knows exactly how his behavior has affected you and he may be more willing to change it.

Don't moralize or lecture. For example, "You should be more considerate of my feelings." When you moralize, you are saying that your morals are superior to the other person's, so you are entitled to tell her how she should behave. This usually offends people and lessens your influence with them.

Don't order or threaten. For example, "If you don't drive more slowly, I'll take the keys." Ordering again implies that you're superior and that offends most people. In fact, orders only seem to work during a threatening situation, and even then only when the threat is present and large. Most people resent being ordered or threatened and may show that they do, at least behind your back.

Don't level on someone else's behalf. For example, "You are putting other drivers at risk." Other people can level for themselves, if they want to. When you do it for them, you are putting them down by implying they can't speak for themselves. You should only level about behavior that has directly affected you.

Don't level on the wrong issue. For example, "You are wasting gas," when your real concern is the reminder of your accident. Sometimes you may feel reluctant to share your real concerns and be tempted to discuss something less personal or threatening. The risk in this is that, if you level on the wrong issue, the other person may give you the wrong change in his behavior.

And I feel "Z"

The "Z" part of the formula should be a clear and accurate report of your feelings. Continuing our example, the complete leveling statement might be "When you drive at eighty in heavy traffic, it reminds me of my accident and I feel anxious and tense." Try to be accurate about both the *nature* and the *strength* of your feelings. If you were feeling angry rather than anxious, you should say "angry." If you were feeling terrified rather than just anxious, you should say "terrified."

Don't level about thoughts instead of feelings. For example, "I feel that I'm going to have another accident." We often use the word "feel" when what we really mean is "think." You are leveling to express your feelings, your emotions, not your thoughts, so make sure the "Z" part of your statement reports feelings. If you say something like "I feel *that* . . ." or "I feel *as if* . . . ," you are probably reporting thoughts and not feelings. If you have not shared your feelings much in the past, you may have trouble recognizing them now. Until you get better at it, it's enough for you to say "I feel bad."

Don't try to keep your feelings to yourself by leaving out the "Z" part of your leveling statement. You may feel embarrassed about sharing your feelings, but remember you really don't have any choice about sharing them, only how constructively you do it. For the sake of your recovery and your relationships, accept any embarrassment and share your feelings constructively.

Don't blame others for your feelings with "you" statements: "You make me frightened." Other people do *not* control your feelings, so they are not responsible for them. Their actions influence how you feel, but so do you by how you think and how you react. Accusations and blaming statements usually make other people defensive and lessen your chances of changing their behavior.

Don't weaken your leveling. For example, "I feel a little anxious" when in fact you feel very anxious. If you make the situation seem unimportant to you, the other person may see it that way, too.

There are three other "don'ts" for effective leveling:

Don't make your leveling statements too long or complicated. For example, "When you drive at eighty in heavy traffic and change lanes and tailgate the car in front so that you have to hit the brakes hard, it reminds me of my accident and I have to close my eyes because I'm getting so anxious and tense that I get a headache and feel like jumping out of the car." If you want the other person to get your message, make it as clear and simple as possible, not a memory test. The times you most need to level are when you feel most upset and neither you nor the other person will cope well with complex messages. The X-Y-Z formula works best when it is simple and clear.

Don't lash out, trying to hurt the other person because she has just hurt you. For example, "You might think I'm stupid being frightened in a car, but how stupid are you, driving like a maniac!" When someone hurts or upsets you, you can feel tempted to lash out. It may give you some short-term satisfaction but only at a cost to the relationship. Usually, the other person did not mean to hurt or upset you. Even if she did, you can handle that more effectively by leveling than by snapping.

Don't level only about bad feelings. If all of the feedback you give other people is negative, you are certainly going to strain their goodwill and affection for you. Eventually, you will lessen your chances of getting them to change their behavior. You may become so unpleasant to them that they begin to avoid you and you lose their emotional support. Level about good feelings as well as bad ones. For example, "I'm feeling a lot better today" or "When you drive at a moderate speed, the ride is much less threatening to me and I feel grateful to you." If you tell someone what he did that made you feel better, then he knows how to make you feel better again.

When not to level

We emphasized that the "Y" part of a leveling statement should describe how the other person's behavior has *directly* affected you. This is often the hardest part of a leveling statement to figure out and many people confuse it with the "Z" part, their feelings. The "Z" part describes the *emotional* effect on you of the other person's behavior, while the "Y" part describes the *direct* effect. Take our example again: "When you drive at eighty in heavy traffic, it reminds me of my accident and I feel anxious and tense." The emotional effect on the speaker is that he feels anxious and tense; the direct effect is that the other person's driving reminds him of his accident.

The best way to find the "Y" part, the direct effect, is to go to your feelings, the "Z" part, and ask yourself, "Why do I feel like that about this behavior?" In our example, you would ask yourself, "Why do I feel anxious and tense when he drives at eighty in heavy traffic?" Your answer would be, "Because it reminds me of my accident." By questioning yourself, you would have found the direct effect of his behavior on you and therefore the "Y" part of your leveling statement.

If you can't find the direct effect on you of the other person's behavior, maybe you shouldn't be using the X-Y-Z formula. It is only appropriate when the other person's behavior has directly affected you in some way. For example, suppose you hear that a friend or relative has been drinking a lot, but not with you or before seeing you. Although her behavior naturally concerns you, it does not *directly* affect you, so it would be inappropriate to level with the X-Y-Z formula. There would be no "Y" part to your statement because you would not be able to say, "Your drinking has this direct effect on me."

In such situations, it may be inappropriate to say anything at all. After all, her behavior is not directly affecting you and you need to think carefully about what right you have to comment on it. On the other hand, it may be triggering strong emotions in you and we encourage you to be open about those. Then we suggest you level about your *opinion*. Like other leveling, try to phrase your statement in "I-language": "Your behavior is none of my business, but I do feel bad about it. Here is what I think about this and here are my reasons." In our sample situation, you might say specifically, "Your drinking is none of my business and I won't discuss it any further if you don't want me to. But I do care about you and I am worried about your drinking. I think having more than four drinks almost every day is not a good idea because medical researchers have found it damages your health." You will be taking the risk that the other person may be offended by your intrusion, no matter how sincere your concern or how good your intentions. So be selective and only level about opinions on issues that trigger strong feelings in you, and only to people who are important to you. People will respect your opinions most if you state them clearly and calmly, if firmly, giving your reasons and using I-language. If you slip into you-language—"*You* have a problem and here's what *you* should do about it"—you are lecturing and lessening your influence, as well as inviting a hostile response.

Practical Exercise

Pause for a few minutes and figure out some leveling statements you could use to tell important people in your life about strong feelings they trigger with their behavior. Use the X-Y-Z formula—"When you did *X*, the effect on me was *Y* and I felt *Z*." If you can't find a direct effect of the other person's behavior on you, think twice about leveling; but, if it's an important issue to you, work out how you can level about your opinion. Practice your leveling statements in your imagination and take the next chance to use them in real life.

Asking for Changes in Behavior

When you have strong feelings, it will sometimes be enough for you to level about them, especially if the person you are talking to listens well and shows his understanding. Sometimes it isn't enough to share your feelings because you also want some change in the situation. This is more likely when your strong feelings have been triggered by the other person's behavior and that's what you would like to change. The most effective way to get someone to change her behavior is to *make a request*.

People are sometimes reluctant to make requests: "I couldn't ask her to do that because she might not want to," or ". . . because he might get angry," or ". . . because she should know what I want." These are all poor reasons for not asking for what you want. The first one implies that people have to accept your requests when, in fact, they can always refuse. The second one says you could not cope if someone gets angry with you. Anger is unpleasant but you would cope, especially if you use a coping statement. The third one implies that other people should be able to read your mind, to guess what you want. If it's important to you, don't leave it to guesswork.

Making Effective Requests

Ineffective requests	Effective requests
❖ "How about some help!" (too vague)	❖ "Would you please pick up my prescription at the pharmacy?" (or another *specific* request for help)
❖ "I want you to show you care more." (vague and unobservable)	❖ "I would like you to ask me how I'm feeling each evening and listen to what I say."
❖ "I don't suppose you want to go out." (negative and vague)	❖ "I would like to go out to a movie tonight."
❖ "I want you to quit telling me how I feel." (negative content)	❖ "Please accept that I know my own feelings."
❖ "Stop moping around or I'll kick you in the behind!" (orders and threats)	❖ "I'd like you to try doing something enjoyable today. Would you like a suggestion?"

Effective requests are *clear and precise*, so the other person knows exactly what you want. Effective requests are for *observable behavior*, so no one can doubt that it happened. Effective requests are made in a *positive and nondefensive manner*, simply by being polite. And effective requests have *positive content*. This means you ask the other person to do something that you want, not to stop doing something that you don't want.

> *Effective requests are clear and precise, so the other person knows exactly what you want.*

If you ask someone to stop doing something, he may try but not know what to do instead. The risk is that he will slip back into the behavior you did not like. You avoid that risk if you ask for what you *do* want instead of the behavior you don't want. For example, instead of asking, "Would you please stop speeding?" you would ask, "Would you please drive at a safe and legal speed?" While you are making a request, try to have some eye contact and speak clearly and audibly. See the box on page 171 for examples of ineffective requests and better alternatives.

Practical Exercise

Pause for a few minutes and figure out some requests you could be making to important people in your life. Follow our guidelines above and look at the examples on page 171. If you want someone to stop doing something, figure out what you want her to do instead, and ask for that. If it's a situation that makes you feel terrible, make sure you level first and then make your request. Practice making your requests in your imagination and then look for chances to use them in real life.

Listening

Listening seems easy, but in fact most people do it poorly. They don't hear what other people are *really* saying and communication breaks down. There is a big difference between hearing and

There is a big difference between hearing and listening.

listening. *Hearing* is a passive process that occurs when your ear picks up any sound that's loud enough and transmits it to your brain. Sometimes you hear sounds you don't want to hear, such as noisy traffic while you're trying to sleep. *Listening*, on the other hand, is an active process with three components. First, you follow what is being said. Second, you interpret what was said. Third, you understand what was said. Without the first two components, you won't get the third.

Listen actively. Try to follow what the other person is saying to you. A simple trick for improving your listening is to pretend to be a tape recorder. Listen as if you'll have to play back what was said to you, without making any important changes. We are not suggesting you actually repeat everything said to you. We are suggesting you set yourself a standard of active listening so that you *could* repeat what was said to you, if you wanted to. If you are not sure you heard what was said, then repeat it back to check it. It shows the other person you are trying to listen and it gives him the chance to correct his message if you did get it wrong. Usually it's enough to focus on being able to play it back, without actually doing so.

Show you are listening. Body language can encourage the other person to communicate with you. Face her and lean toward her a little, rather than facing or leaning away. Keep a comfortable distance between you, not too close and not too distant. Try to have eye contact about half the time.

Don't interrupt, even if you strongly disagree with what he's saying. Your guess about what he was going to say next might be wrong and interrupting is denying the other person the right to say his piece. Listening to someone does not necessarily mean you agree with him; it only shows you respect his right to have his say. You can disagree *after* listening, if you want to.

Don't do all the talking. If you are the crisis victim, you will need to talk about your feelings from time to time. But your experience and your feelings also affect the feelings of important people in your life and they need a chance to level, too.

Don't hide behind furniture or your "body armor." If you put barriers, such as kitchen tables or desks, between you and the other person, he will feel like you are keeping him at a distance and will communicate less. *Body armor* means hiding behind folded arms and crossed legs, making your body into a rigid, emotional fortress. Try to have a relaxed and open posture.

Interpret thoughtfully. Try to work out the real meaning of what is being said to you. Think about whether something more is behind the obvious message. If you think there might be, don't rely on your guess but ask the other person to see if your guess was right. For example, "Okay, I understand you are telling me it wastes gas to drive quickly, but it sounds to me like something else is on your mind. Is that right?" You have done as much as you can by inviting her to level on what she sees as the real issue.

Validating

Validating means accepting that what the other person said is true for him. He is accurately telling you how he feels. If you think about it, you can't really do anything *but* validate. After all, why would you know how he feels better than he does? Validating should be easy, and it is certainly simple. The basic formula is always "I understand that's how you feel." For example, if someone told you, "When you drive at eighty in heavy traffic, it reminds me of my accident and that makes me feel tense and anxious," to validate her feelings you would reply, "Okay, I understand that makes you feel tense and anxious."

Notice that you are only saying, "I understand that's *how* you feel." You are not necessarily saying, "I understand *why* you feel

> *Notice that you are only saying, "I understand that's how you feel." You are not necessarily saying, "I understand why you feel like that."*

like that." If you honestly think you understand why the other person feels as he said, then say so. This usually means you would feel the same way if you were in his shoes. Sometimes you won't understand why the other person is feeling as he says he feels, and it's not necessary that you do. It's enough if you accept that's how he feels. So you might say, "Okay, I understand that's how you feel. It's not how I would feel, but I see it's how you feel."

Validating is the final important step in sharing feelings constructively. When you validate someone, you are showing you understand and accept her feelings and this will help her to accept them, too. So validate clearly, promptly and nondefensively.

Don't insist others should feel like you do: "Well, I wouldn't feel frightened at that speed." You should show you understand and accept her feelings, not try to control them.

Don't defend your actions when they have an effect you didn't intend. For example, "Well, I didn't mean to scare you with my driving." If you didn't mean to scare the other person, then you have nothing to defend. Often, your effect on someone else is not what you intended, and that can put you under pressure to justify your actions. It's more helpful to explain your intentions and still validate her feelings: "I certainly didn't mean to scare you with my driving, but I can see that I did."

Don't dodge the issue by avoiding what is obviously the other person's main concern to discuss something that is more interesting or more comfortable for you. Replying to our example leveling statement with "Well, I suppose the traffic was heavy today," when you know it was your driving that upset the other person, is an example of dodging.

Don't tell other people to "be logical." For example, "You really should stop worrying now. There's no logical reason for it anymore." Humans don't usually think as logically as a computer. We tend to think plausibly. If something seems plausible or believable to us, we usually accept it. There are always plausible reasons for people's reactions, even if the reactions seem illogical to an outside observer. If you tell someone to stop feeling bad because her reactions seem illogical to you, she may then feel stupid (hardly an improvement!) and just stop telling you how she feels (not exactly good communication!).

> *There are always plausible reasons for people's reactions, even if the reactions seem illogical to an outside observer.*

Don't reassure someone who is feeling bad. For example, "I understand why you are worried about your sick daughter, but I'm sure she will be all right." Reassuring troubled people is always meant to be helpful, but it really just tells them they are being stupid to feel bad because you know everything will turn out fine in the end. The likely effect is to block communication, and you are going to look silly if your confident prediction turns out wrong.

> *Telling people to "be logical" about their bad feelings and offering them reassurance are two common ways of encouraging people to deny their natural feelings.*

Telling people to "be logical" about their bad feelings and offering them reassurance are two common ways of encouraging people to deny their natural feelings. If you are the victim of a crisis, people with the best of intentions may do both to you, along with encouragement to "Forget about it now." We encourage you to resist these misguided attempts to be helpful. If necessary, level and make a request: for example, "When you tell me my fears are illogical, you're telling me how I should feel, and that just makes me feel stupid. I would rather you accept that my feelings are normal for someone who's been through my experience."

Don't bring up the past. People usually do this to defend their own actions: "Well, you used to drive pretty fast yourself." If the other person did something that upset you in the past, you should have leveled about it then. Right now, you should be showing you understand and accept her feelings, not defending yourself. The other practical point here is to level right away. As soon as someone does something that strongly affects your feelings, good or bad, level immediately or at least as soon as possible.

Body Talk

We have been focusing on *what* to say to share feelings constructively. At least as important, if not more so, is *how* you say it. Effective communication means you speak clearly and audibly. The tone of your voice will indicate your true feelings, so keep your leveling honest, too. Don't send confusing and contradictory messages by saying something in a tone that suggests something different. You also send messages through your body posture and movement. To repeat, communication works better if you face and lean a little toward the other person, keeping eye contact about half the time. If you look relaxed, it helps the other person to relax.

Don't send confusing and contradictory messages by saying something in a tone that suggests something different.

In addition to using your own body talk to communicate, you can look at the other person's body talk for clues about how he is feeling. Look at the expression on his face, how his body is positioned and how he moves. Listen to the way he is speaking. But don't kid yourself about how accurately you can read body talk. Despite what some pop psychologists may try to sell you, body talk gives *clues* about feelings, not absolute indications. To understand a nonverbal clue, you need to understand a lot about the other person, her cultural background and the immediate situation. So check your guess by asking the other person what she feels. For example, "You look upset about this. Would you like to tell me how you're feeling?" You have done your best by inviting her to level.

But This Is So Artificial!

"Leveling, listening, validating, watching how I sit and where I look. I thought good communication just came naturally." No, it doesn't. "Natural" is a misused word. It means "without outside influence" and it's impossible for human beings to grow up without some outside influences, from family, friends, school and society. You have been trained in communication, whether you noticed it or not. The problem for many of us is that the communication habits we learned don't really help us handle strong feelings effectively. Most of the time, people try to deny or belittle their strong feelings. When that doesn't work, we slip into the other extreme and exaggerate them. Neither of these popular, "natural" approaches is going to help you handle the strong feelings triggered by your crisis.

So it's time for some relearning. Yes, that will feel artificial, awkward, even "unnatural," but only at first. We have taught these communication skills to individuals, couples, families, business and work groups. Everybody struggles with it in the beginning, but with a little practice and application, it becomes their new "natural" way of sharing feelings and it works better than what they did before. If you have been lucky enough to learn these skills in the past, just remind yourself to use them now to help you cope with your crisis. Sometimes the depression occurring during recovery tempts people to bottle up and withdraw, slowing recovery and straining relationships. If you have not previously had the chance to learn communication skills, now is your chance. They will be helpful long after you have completed your recovery. See the box below for examples of ineffective communication and some better alternatives.

Effective Communication

Ineffective communication	Effective communication
❖ Interrupting	❖ Listen actively; wait your turn; be brief.
❖ Making accusations; blaming	❖ Level with an X-Y-Z statement.
❖ Overgeneralizing ("You always . . ." or "You never . . .")	❖ Focus on this situation.
❖ Lecturing ("You should . . ." or "You must . . .")	❖ Make a request or offer a suggestion.
❖ Hogging the conversation	❖ Take turns talking; be brief.
❖ Sidetracking (getting off the current issue)	❖ Stick to one issue at a time; raise others later.
❖ Bringing up the past	❖ Stick to the present; it's too late to change the past.
❖ Deliberately trying to hurt someone	❖ Use a coping statement for your own hurt, then level.

Practical Exercise

If you have had trouble sharing your feelings effectively in any of your important relationships, you will find it easier to try out the suggestions in this chapter if you work on it together with the other person in that relationship. If he has learned about listening and validating, he will know how to respond helpfully whenever you level. If he has learned about leveling, he will know how to share his feelings effectively. Of course, it's then up to you to listen and validate. Even if it feels awkward, try some practice sessions together for up to half an hour each. Then you will be more likely to remember how to use the skills when strong feelings occur.

10

Coping with the Big Three: Depression, Anger, Guilt

The two most common emotional reactions during recovery from a crisis are depression and anger. They can occur for years after the crisis, at disruptive levels, particularly in victims who have not received counseling. A third common emotional reaction is guilt, usually occurring when a victim, such as the driver in a car accident, believes that he was partly or completely responsible for the crisis. In previous chapters we outline the basic approach to managing all bad feelings, including these three, and we refer to those chapters from time to time. But these three feelings are so common in crisis victims and can be so disruptive that we now want to give you more specific information and suggestions about each.

Depression

Occasional feelings of depression are normal: They happen to just about everybody and are not a reason for concern. It is certainly common for crisis victims to feel depressed during the recovery phase. You may be able to cope with your natural feelings of depression by using a coping statement (see chapter 8) and keeping yourself occupied. Depression becomes a problem when it is intense, lasts for long periods of time and interferes with your normal functioning. If you aren't sure whether you have a problem with depression, try to answer the following questions.

- Do you often feel sad, low or blue?

- Are you doing much less than you used to?

- Do you get along with people worse than you used to?

- Do you often feel guilty?

- Do you see your problems as too big to tackle?

- Do you doubt that things will ever improve?

- Are you having trouble sleeping?

- Do you feel tired most of the time?

- Is your appetite worse than it used to be?

- Have you lost interest in sex?

- Do you think of suicide?

The more of these questions you answered "Yes" to, the more depressed you probably are and the more important it is that you try to do something constructive about it. So, what can you do?

Physical treatments for depression

A doctor may suggest a physical treatment for your depression, most likely drugs. We realize that when you're depressed, you don't feel like thinking or making decisions, but we would be letting you down if we did not share our reservations about drug treatment and offer you an alternative.

Psychiatrists evaluating antidepressants found that 20 to 40 percent of depressed patients were not helped by them. Of those who did improve, many refused to continue taking the drugs or developed side-effects that either prevented them from continuing or required an additional drug to offset the effects. Of those successfully treated with these drugs, up to 50 percent relapsed into depression again within a year of stopping the drug. Overall, not a stunning record of success.

As psychologists, we are *not* simply opposed to drugs. In the past we have ourselves conducted research on combined drug and psychology treatment programs. We *are* opposed to people taking drugs, especially for long periods, simply to anesthetize themselves

against bad feelings that are the understandable reaction to
something in their lives, such as a crisis experience. If you are
already finding antidepressant drugs helpful, or if your doctor
suggests you try them, that's fine by us. What we suggest is that
you also learn how to manage your depression for yourself so that
you don't need to rely on those drugs for the rest of your life.

The causes of depression

Experts are still debating whether there are different kinds of
depression, with some kinds caused by internal, possibly biological
problems that require biological treatment. This argument won't
concern us here because your depression has most likely been
triggered by your crisis experience and the following theory of
depression probably explains yours. In this theory, there are three
possible causes of depression.

First, depression can result from a lack of rewards from life.
This may be a direct result of your crisis. For example, if your crisis
was the death of a close relative or friend, then you have lost the
rewards of that relationship, or if your crisis has kept you away
from your job, you may be missing the rewards of work. Your lack
of rewards may be an indirect result of your crisis: For example,
if your post-crisis depression has led to low activity levels on your
part, then you won't be doing much that could give you rewards.

Second, depression can result from too much punishment in
your life. For crisis victims, the crisis itself tends to have been a big
and unexpected punishment. If it has left you in pain or in difficult
circumstances, that punishment may be continuing.

Third, depression can result from unrealistically negative
thinking. These negative thoughts tend to be of three kinds, also.

1. Depressed people often engage in a lot of self-criticism
   and self-blaming.

2. They often interpret present events in negative ways.

3. They tend to have negative expectations about the
   future—it's never going to get any better and they
   will never be able to cope again.

Negative thinking like this is common for crisis victims, which probably explains why depression is such a common feature of the recovery stage. As we described in chapter 1, one of the main psychological effects of a crisis experience is to destroy our belief that we are invulnerable and that the world is a safe and predictable place. Ronnie Janoff-Bulman, a psychologist at the University of Massachusetts who has been researching crisis reactions, suggests that those beliefs begin early in life, possibly as young as two or three years old. She suggests that these beliefs lead a child to see herself as worthy of a safe life and so the beliefs become a part of her self-esteem. When a person suffers a crisis, not only her beliefs in personal invulnerability and a fair and predictable world are shattered but, as a result, her sense of self-worth is also damaged. So some crisis victims come to see the world as a dangerous or threatening place and blame themselves for events for which they were only partly responsible or not responsible at all. You will recognize in these reactions some of the key elements of depressive thinking described above: self-blame, self-criticism and a negative view of the present and the future.

This is not meant to be a lecture on depression theory. If you understand what is causing your depression, you have targets for reducing it to a more reasonable level: by making sure you are getting enough rewards from life, by coping with the problems in your life and by making your thinking as realistic as possible.

Managing your depression

Following is a basic self-help program for managing depression. After you have read it, if you are too overwhelmed even to start, or if you try it and it doesn't help, consider getting professional help. Depression is a common but potentially serious problem, especially for crisis victims. You don't have to just suffer through it.

Depression is a common but potentially serious problem, especially for crisis victims. You don't have to just suffer through it.

Step 1: Record your mood level. A small, spiral-bound notebook is most convenient for this. It's easy to write in and will slip into a pocket or bag. Start a new page for each day and record noticeable changes in your mood level, along with the associated activity or situation and your thoughts at the time. You can record your mood on a scale of 0 (no depression at all) to 7 (as depressed as you could be). An example might look like this:

Tuesday

10:30 A.M. Depression = 4. Standing behind the bank counter, serving customers, thinking, "I'll never feel safe at work again."

7:00 P.M. Depression = 6. Sitting on the couch at home doing nothing, thinking, "I'm never going to enjoy life again. No one understands how terrible I feel."

Step 2: Record your daily activities. Keep a record of your major regular activities. You don't need to record brushing your teeth or other small activities, just the main ones. You can do this in the diary you have started for recording your mood levels by including a brief description of your activities. Within the example we started above, you might find records like these:

3:00 P.M. Finishing account books for the day. Depression = 3
8:00 P.M. Playing softball. Depression = 2

Using these two steps (recording your mood level and recording your daily activities), you should be able to identify the major influences on your mood level, how you are spending most of your time and how you feel as a result of those activities.

Step 3: Identify your present rewards. Humans generally need two kinds of rewards to feel and function well. We need enjoyable experiences, those that lift our mood, and we need experiences of mastery, activities that we see as worth doing and that we think we do reasonably well. Review the activities you have recorded in your diary to identify how many of both kinds of rewards you are currently getting out of life. If an activity gave you any pleasure, put a capital "P" next to it. If an activity gave you any sense of mastery, put a capital "M" next to it. Be fair to yourself when you do this review. Because depressed people are self-critical, they won't always acknowledge their mastery experiences.

Step 4: Do you need more rewards? When you have a reasonable sample of your present activities, for at least a typical week in your life, count up the Ms and Ps you have recorded. Are you getting enough? Of both kinds? On most days? Or are there gaps in your rewards that need to be filled? If you identify a lack of pleasure or achievement in your present lifestyle, your next step is to plan to fill that gap. Can you revive activities that used to be rewarding? Do you need to find new ones? Do you need help to find some?

Keep in mind that if your activity level has severely dropped, you can't expect to rebuild it instantly. A long list of new activities might overwhelm you and scare you out of starting even one of them. You are more likely to succeed if you build up rewarding activities in gradual steps. Try one or two new or renewed activities until you are managing them comfortably, and then add one or two more. Also keep in mind that new activities may require new skills, so you may need to get some help learning them.

Step 5: Do you need to reduce the punishment in your life? By now, the actual crisis is probably over so there is nothing you can do about it. If you are still coping with a prolonged crisis, make sure you are taking all the practical steps possible to manage it. Either way, has your crisis created other problems for you? Or are there other problems in your life, not related to your crisis, that clearly contribute to your depression? Situations you have recorded in your diary that trigger big drops in your mood level may represent problems for you. Write a list of the current problems in your life, your present sources of punishment. Then go through it and rank them in order of their importance and how much control you have over them. Which ones are urgent or make a big difference in your life, that you can do something about now? The idea is to start where you can get some worthwhile results.

Self-reward is an excellent antidepressant and important encouragement to keep you going.

Once you have your problems ranked, tackle them, starting with number one. If it looks too big to tackle, break it down into steps and tackle one step at a time. Give yourself a well-earned pat on the back as you tackle each problem or step. Self-reward is an excellent antidepressant and important encouragement to keep you going. You may decide you need help tackling some problems. Fine; go get it.

Step 6: Make your thinking more realistic. Look through your diary for the thoughts associated with big drops or low points in your mood level. Using the steps outlined in chapter 8, challenge those thoughts by finding the thinking mistakes in them and the underlying irrational beliefs. Using the rational ideas in chapter 8, work out a more rational view of the situation and try to think that way the next time it happens. Don't be surprised if you don't believe this rational view at first; most depressed people don't. It takes repeated challenging of your unrealistically negative thoughts, plus the constructive actions of building your rewards and tackling your problems, before you really believe your new way of thinking.

We have described step six only briefly because it is explained in detail in chapter 8, but don't underestimate its importance. Straight thinking is an important part of managing your bad feelings, including depression.

Suicide?

Many depressed people have thoughts about suicide and some attempt it, sometimes successfully. They are more likely to try it when they feel especially hopeless about the future: "Not only is my life a mess now, it's never going to get any better." You may have thoughts of suicide, so let's discuss it.

We are not automatically opposed to the idea of suicide. We can imagine some circumstances in which it might be a reasonable option, such as having an incurable, painful and progressive illness that makes you a burden to your family. Situations like these are at the center of the current debate about euthanasia. The problem with suicide is that most of the people who consider it seriously are really not in such desperate and unworkable situations. At the time, they *believe* they are and that's why suicide seems a plausible solution to them. It seems to offer the only end to their suffering. That assessment of both their situation and future is a clear example of the unrealistically negative thinking of a depressed person.

People who make genuine attempts at suicide but survive usually decide later that their attempt was a mistake.

People who make genuine attempts at suicide but survive usually decide later that their attempt was a mistake. They understand why it made sense at the time, because of how they were feeling and thinking, but later they realize how mistaken their thinking was. The mistake rate in choosing suicide is very high. The problem is, if your suicide was successful, it's impossible to undo.

We encourage depressed people to see suicide as a possible option, with its own pros and cons: immediate end to your suffering, but hurt to those left behind, total loss of future enjoyment and so on. Then we suggest you consider your other options because there always are some. Because of the high chance that choosing suicide will actually be a mistake for you, as it is for most people, it makes sense for you to try some of your other options first, building up your rewards and tackling your problems, however difficult that may seem when you're depressed. If you are seriously considering suicide, we strongly encourage you to investigate your options, with help if you need it.

Anger

During their recovery, many crisis victims have periods of anger. Sometimes this anger is focused, with more or less justification, at someone or something the victim sees as having caused or contributed to his crisis experience. Sometimes it is less focused because there is no one and nothing to blame for the crisis. In either case, it is often directed toward family, friends or associates, because they are available as targets while the perceived causes of the crisis may not be. This places strain on the victim's relationships and may further isolate him from valuable support.

Yet anger is a normal human emotion and a common reaction during recovery from a crisis. In a way, victims are angry at the blow fate has dealt them, which is understandable. A healthy recovery involves accepting the normality of your emotional reactions so that you can work through them. Try to accept and express your anger in ways that are not unnecessarily harmful to you or your relationships. That's what anger management is about.

What is anger?

Anger is the emotional response you feel when you are provoked. It is a *feeling* and should not be confused with aggression, which is a *behavior*, behavior that is intended to hurt, harm or at least frighten. Anger does not have to lead to aggression, even though it often does. Anger can have both positive and negative

> *Anger does not have to lead to aggression, even though it often does.*

functions. It can energize you. It can push you into expressing yourself. It can be an important cue that you are facing a problem. And it can make you feel more powerful, more able to tackle the problem. On the negative side, excessive anger disrupts your behavior and often makes it less effective. It can be defensive on your part, blocking effective communication. Sadly, it often prompts aggression, a behavior that rarely gets you what you want and always damages you and your relationships. The purpose of anger management is to gain the positive functions of anger while avoiding the negative ones.

When is anger a problem?

Occasional feelings of anger are normal and happen to all of us when we are provoked. Some anger is a normal part of the crisis recovery cycle. So how do you know when anger is becoming a problem? Try answering the following questions:

- Do you get angry often?
- When you get angry, do you get extremely angry?
- When you get angry, do you stay angry?
- When you get angry, do you act aggressively?
- Does your anger interfere with your work?

- Does your anger interfere with your relationships?

- Has your anger affected your health?

The more times you answered "Yes," the more likely it is that you are having a problem with anger and it is time you did something constructive about it. To start, figure out the causes of your anger, so you can tackle them. There are three general causes of anger: external factors, internal factors and your behavior. We describe each of these so that you can identify which apply to you.

External causes of anger

The external causes of anger are the situations or events that spark it. Different people are provoked by different things, but there are four common kinds of provocation leading to anger. *Frustrations* are situations in which your actions are blocked in some way, so that you are unable to achieve your immediate goals. *Annoyances* and *irritations* are the things that get on your nerves, depending on your likes and dislikes. *Abuse* may be verbal or physical, but none of us like either kind. And *injustice* or *unfairness* can trigger anger, including the feeling held by many victims that their crisis experience was undeserved and unfair. In principle, the thing to do about provocative situations is to try to handle them constructively.

Internal causes of anger

In general, your habitual thoughts and emotions are internal causes of anger. Your *thinking habits* include how you usually size up situations and how you usually expect things to turn out. Do you see provocations where they don't exist, such as thinking someone is picking on you when he isn't? Do you exaggerate the provocations that do exist, like overreacting to something that was just a joke? Do you expect to lose badly if you don't stick up for yourself? In principle, the antidote for unrealistic thinking habits is to build realistic thinking habits, as explained in chapter 8.

> *In principle, the antidote for tension and agitation is to be able to relax, mentally and physically.*

Your emotional habits are the moods you usually keep yourself in. Bad moods certainly set you up to overreact to provocations. If you are tense or agitated most of the time, it won't take much to make you angry. In principle, the antidote for tension and agitation is to be able to relax, mentally and physically. When you are already angry, it is easy to exaggerate the provocations in your life. Prolonged anger gives you an ideal opportunity to use the mental relaxation technique described in chapter 8. Keep in mind that you should also learn how to relax physically. If you are always depressed, the only other emotion you may be able to muster is anger. See page 182 for ways to work on long-lasting depression.

The other emotional aid you can use to manage your anger is your sense of humor. If you are honest with yourself, you'll see that many of the situations that bother you also have their funny side. Sometimes the funny side is you, if you are willing to recognize when you are indulging in false pride or overinflated dignity. As soon as you can laugh at a situation, you detach from it emotionally, so it will have less impact on you. Humor also has a calming effect. You can't go wrong if you deliberately look for the funny side of provocative situations.

Behavioral causes of anger

Being submissive or being aggressive in response to provocation are two ways of behaving that will likely increase your anger.

Being *submissive* involves withdrawal or avoidance, either walking out of the situation or dodging it altogether. It means you go away mad instead of dealing with the incident. The risk is that you then stew over it, making yourself angrier. As a part of this stewing, you may blame yourself for not handling the situation better and so lose self-esteem with the further risk that you then become depressed.

> *Being submissive or being aggressive in response to provocation are two ways of behaving that will likely increase your anger.*

Aggression means behavior intended to hurt or frighten, a selfish attempt to get what you want regardless of how you affect others. Being aggressive often provokes an aggressive reaction so that the conflict, and your anger, escalate. Often you get stuck in a long, unsolvable conflict, unless you back down and lapse into being submissive. Even when your aggression seems to have won, it has been at major costs to you. You probably stayed angry to win, and there is now good evidence linking high levels of anger with heart disease, especially competitive anger. Your relationships suffer because no one likes or respects a bully. In principle, the antidote to submission and aggression is to learn how to deal with provocations assertively.

> *Responsible assertion involves dealing with other people on a basis of mutual respect.*

Responsible *assertion* involves dealing with other people on a basis of mutual respect. You show you respect their rights and feelings, but without surrendering your own rights or suffering unnecessarily bad feelings yourself, including anger. To deal assertively with a confrontation, you may use effective communication (see chapter 9), assertive expression of your opinions, negotiation or problem-solving skills.

Managing your anger

By now you should have a reasonable idea of which common factors are contributing to your anger and you will have noticed our suggestions for what to do about each, in principle. Now let's translate those suggestions into a practical plan for managing your anger.

Step 1: Accept responsibility for your anger level. As we explained in chapter 8, factors outside you *influence* how you feel but they don't *control* it. Provocations influence your anger, but they don't control it. You have a big say in how angry you get, how often and how long it lasts, depending on how you think and what you do about your provocations. So it's up to you to monitor your own anger level, to recognize when it's going up and begin some constructive action then. The earlier you manage your anger, the easier it is. If you wait until you are furious, it's harder to act sensibly—although that's not an excuse for not trying.

Step 2: Practice and use the calming response. One of the reasons anger can be a problem is that it often builds up quickly. One minute you feel more or less okay, the next you are furious and have trouble reacting constructively. This is exactly the situation in which the calming response is helpful, for slowing down your emotional reaction and restoring your sense of self-control. We have given you detailed instructions for the calming response at the end of chapter 8 (see page 152). If you have not already started practicing it, but you are having a problem with anger, then go back and learn it now. Start looking for early warning signs of anger, so that you remind yourself to use the calming response as soon as you can. Practice it and use it.

Step 3: Strengthen your realistic thinking habits. As a provocation occurs, a calming response may be all you need to keep your anger at a reasonable level. If it isn't, use the breathing space created by the calming response to say a coping statement to yourself. Perhaps something like this: "I expect to feel angry (in response to this provocation) but I'll cope; I won't deny my anger but I also won't dwell on it; if possible, I'll do something constructive to tackle this provocation; if not, I'll do something else, pleasant or constructive, to distract me." And then make sure you *do* try to tackle the problem constructively, if possible, or do something else to distract you if not.

As soon as you can after the event (or even better, *before* the event, if you can predict a coming provocation), figure out what your thoughts are about the situation and test them for thinking mistakes and irrational beliefs. Then work out a more rational view of the situation so that in the future it does not make you any more angry than it has to. This is a summary of the mental relaxation procedure we explain in chapter 8. If you are not already practicing it but you are having a problem with anger, go back now and learn it. Recurring provocations in your life are an ideal opportunity to do a full, written mental relaxation exercise.

Step 4: Express your anger constructively. After you get your anger to a reasonable level, try to express it constructively. This means that eventually you feel better, no one else feels unnecessarily bad and you may have changed the situation more to your liking. The two most likely ways of achieving this will be to level about your anger, then request a change in someone else's behavior. If you want her to understand and accept how you feel, show your willingness to do the same by listening actively and validating her feelings. You will recognize this short list of communication and assertion skills from our detailed description in chapter 9. If you are not already practicing them but you do have a problem with anger, go back and learn them now.

Stopping arguments

The most likely way your anger could cause problems for your relationships is to cause a lot of arguments. Arguments are destructive outbursts of bad feelings. You are expressing your bad feelings, but in ways that are destructive for the relationship. Arguments are often attempts to manipulate each other, to make someone do what you want, regardless of what he wants. If you think about it, you will realize arguments result from a lack of communication and assertion skills. The real answer is to strengthen and use good communication and assertion instead of arguing. In the short term, however, you can also take some practical steps to stop arguments, so that you can switch to more effective communication and assertion instead. If your anger has been leading to a lot of arguments, you can usefully extend your anger-management program with the following steps.

The earlier one of you takes a constructive initiative, the easier it is to avoid a stupid argument.

Step 1: If an argument looms, stop the conversation. The person who is getting angry should accept this responsibility but, if she doesn't, the other person can. Someone should have the sense to do it. Look for the early warning signs of an argument, such as increasing tension, rising volumes and the tendency to talk over each other.

The earlier one of you takes a constructive initiative, the easier it is to avoid a stupid argument. As soon as you realize an argument is on the way or has already started, say something like "Hold it! I'm getting upset [or, you look as if you're getting upset]. If we go on like this, we will end up having an argument and arguments are silly. Can we stop for a minute?"

Step 2: Can you communicate better now? For the moment, stop thinking about *what* you were discussing and focus on *how* you were discussing it. Could you be communicating better? Should one of you be leveling? Should one of you be listening and validating? Can you pick up the conversation again using better communication skills? Or is one or both of you too angry for that now?

Step 3: If too angry, take time out to cool down. If you or the other person is too angry to communicate constructively, take time out from the conversation to cool down. This does not mean just walking out, which usually makes the other person even angrier. Taking time out means you make a clear commitment to return to the discussion when everyone has cooled down. So you might say something like this: "I'm too angry [or, you're too angry] for us to discuss this now without an argument. I suggest we take a half hour to cool down." Or pick a specific time to discuss it later, a time that will suit you both: "Let's discuss it tonight after dinner."

If you take time out, use it to cool down. If you sit around stewing over the situation in unrealistically negative ways, you will just increase your anger. Use realistic thinking to manage your anger and to figure out what you really want from the situation and the most effective way of going after that. Then try to stick to that plan when you return to the discussion. These steps for stopping arguments are easier to use if all of the people in the situation know them so they can respond constructively when you take a constructive initiative. If arguments have become a problem in an important relationship, share the skills with the other person by asking her to read this

It takes two to fight and there is no value in letting yourself be drawn into an argument.

section. Then offer to try to use them and ask her to try, too. If someone you are trying not to argue with refuses your constructive initiative and wants to keep arguing, refuse. It takes two to fight and there is no value in letting yourself be drawn into an argument. Stick to your constructive initiative by saying something like, "I'm sorry you are so angry that you want to argue now, but I see no good coming from an argument. I do want to sort out this problem with you and I'll be available to discuss it when you have cooled down. Right now, I'm going to leave the situation so that we can cool down."

And leave. It may take willpower and you may receive a load of verbal abuse, but it's better than useless, destructive arguments.

Guilt

In addition to depression and anger, some crisis victims experience a lot of guilt. This may result from their belief that they caused or contributed to the crisis: for example, the driver in a road accident, the skipper in a boating disaster, the leader of a lost hiking group and so on. In some cases, the belief that you triggered or contributed to the crisis may be realistic—you can identify an action of yours that was clearly related to the cause of the crisis. You may have been speeding. You may have failed to check that lifejackets were on board. You may have underestimated the difficulty of a planned walk. In a surprising number of cases, self-blaming is downright unrealistic, like blaming yourself for going into a bank at the time it was being held up. Regardless of how realistic this thinking is, however, it causes guilt.

If you feel excessively guilty, you are probably judging yourself unrealistically, and dealing with that is the key to managing your guilt.

Sometimes guilt results from a victim's actions during and in response to the crisis. As we described in chapter 1, the fourth stage of the crisis response is a non-emotional survival state, in which your thinking is narrowly focused on survival at all costs. During this stage, people sometimes take actions for their personal survival that they feel ashamed of later, like the survivor of a crowd crush at a British football match who later recalled walking on other people's heads to escape.

Guilt is a normal emotional response, like depression and anger, so it also reflects how you think about the situation. When you feel guilty, you are saying something to yourself like, "My behavior was wrong and bad. I have broken my own moral code." If you feel excessively guilty, you are probably judging yourself unrealistically, and dealing with that is the key to managing your guilt.

Step 1: Try to judge yourself fairly. How realistic is your belief that you caused or contributed to your crisis? It may be clear-cut and in that case you have to cope with your legitimate guilt. But stop to think about it. The risk is that right now you are also depressed, not thinking too straight, and inclined to blame yourself unrealistically. Are you blaming yourself when there is really no evidence to support that conclusion (thinking mistake number three)? Are you blaming yourself for a situation that resulted from other people's actions, too (thinking mistake number six)?

> *It's easy to be wise after an event. It's human to be fixated on your personal survival during a crisis.*

How realistic is your belief that you should have acted differently during the crisis? Remember, the non-emotional survival state is the *normal* human reaction during a crisis. It's how most people react. Don't be put down by smart alecs who weren't there asking you why you didn't act differently. Odds are, they would have acted just as you did, if they had been in your shoes. It's easy to be wise after an event. It's human to be fixated on your personal survival during a crisis.

Step 2: Say a coping statement to yourself. Whenever you experience peaks of guilt, manage them by saying a coping statement. This time it might go like this: "I expect to feel guilty when I remember what I did, but I'll cope with feeling guilty. I won't try to deny my guilt because I do think what I did was wrong, but I won't help anybody by making myself feel rotten by dwelling on it. If possible, I'll do something constructive now to undo the effects of my actions. If that's not possible, I'll do something else, pleasant or constructive, to distract me."

> *In the end, you will have to accept your regrets as a part of the ugly memory your crisis will become.*

Sometimes you have a chance to do something that *does* directly undo at least some of the effects of your behavior. You may be able to atone in some way. Usually, however, you won't be able to directly undo the effects of your behavior. You may satisfy your sense of justice by compensating in some other way, such as working for a charity or doing some community work. In the end, you will have to accept your regrets as a part of the ugly memory your crisis will become.

Step 3: Accept your human imperfection. Underlying excessive guilt you will usually find irrational belief number two, the one that says, "I must be completely competent and make no mistakes if I am to be worthwhile." The alternative rational idea says, "Like everybody, I will occasionally fail or make a mistake. Then I will feel bad, but I can cope with that, and I can take constructive steps to do better next time." You may have made real mistakes in your crisis and you will always regret them, but to have made mistakes only makes you human.

Excessive guilt can also reflect irrational belief number three, if you apply it to yourself: "Some people are bad or wicked, and they should be blamed or punished for this." The alternative rational idea could be applied to guilt like this: "It is sad that I may have done some bad things, but making myself feel rotten won't change that." Some constructive plans for behavioral change are more likely to help than beating yourself up ever will.

If you have tried to judge your behavior as objectively as you can and you still conclude that some part of it was wrong, in your own eyes, then the only realistic response is to feel guilty. As a part of laying your crisis to rest as a permanently bad memory, you may have to accept some regrets about part of your behavior.

"I expect to regret what I did on that occasion, but I'll cope with those regrets. I won't deny them because I think I deserve them, but I won't exaggerate them by dwelling on the past because that doesn't help anybody. If there is anything I can do to undo or compensate for the effects of my behavior, I'll try to do it. Otherwise the best thing I can do is get on with my life and try to behave better if I ever find myself in a similar situation."

Notice that we are not suggesting you give yourself license to behave any way at all in the future; we are suggesting you forgive yourself for how you may have behaved in the past.

Step 4: Share your guilt constructively. We have already suggested that, having accepted the normality of your emotional reactions to your crisis, you share them constructively because you will share them anyway, nonverbally if not verbally. The same advice applies to guilt. *Guilt* is the bad feeling that results from judging yourself as having been bad. *Shame* is the bad feeling that results from thinking other people will judge you as bad. Many people increase their guilt by trying to keep it to themselves because they fear the shame they expect to feel if they tell others about their guilt. "What will other people think of me if I tell them how I feel, or what I did?"

Again we encourage you to share your strong feelings, including guilt, constructively by leveling. There are two big advantages to this. First, others will probably look more objectively than you at your actions and help you recognize when you are blaming yourself unfairly or unrealistically. Second, others may agree that your actions were wrong but show that your actions don't change how they feel about you. Your *value* as a human being comes from your being human and is neither increased nor diminished by any of your actions. They can be judged for themselves. If you bite the bullet and share your guilt with someone, you may be pleasantly surprised at how supportive it is when he shows he can understand and share your regrets about your behavior while still feeling love and respect for you. His understanding and forgiveness might be a good example for you to apply to yourself.

11

Sleeping Better

Insomnia, or disturbed sleep, is a common reaction to a crisis. It may be the most obvious symptom of distress in victims who did not receive supportive counseling and who are trying to deny their crisis reactions. In children who have trouble talking about their experience or reactions, disturbed sleep may be the most obvious sign of how disturbed they are. Sometimes the link with the crisis is obvious because your sleep is disturbed by memories or nightmares of the crisis itself. Sometimes the link is not so obvious but, if you used to sleep okay before the crisis and now you don't, your psychological reactions to the crisis are probably contributing to your new sleeping problem. Sleeping problems are actually very common—up to a third of adults have trouble sleeping at any given time and up to a fifth have serious sleeping problems. It's possible that your crisis has worsened a sleeping problem you already had.

Insomnia is not a life-threatening problem, so it is not always taken seriously. If your sleep is disturbed, however, you know just how disruptive it can be. *Insomnia* is defined as poor sleep accompanied by daytime fatigue. This includes being physically tired, having trouble concentrating, feeling depressed, irritable or lethargic. These daytime components of insomnia are the real problem and an unwanted additional obstacle to your recovery from your crisis.

> *Insomnia is not a life-threatening problem, so it is not always taken seriously.*

What Is Sleep?

Sleep is more than just not being awake. There are five different levels of sleep, which can be distinguished from each other by the patterns of electrical activity occurring in the brain during each level. Levels one through four consist of light to very deep sleep and are characterized by a gradual smoothening of the electrical activity. People normally move back and forth through these levels during sleep. We usually reach level four, the deepest, a couple of hours after falling asleep.

Level five is the strange sleep phase because it is marked by electrical activity in the brain similar to that of someone who is awake. The sleeper's eyes move rapidly under her closed eyelids, which is why this level is sometimes called REM (rapid eye movement) sleep. Yet her body muscles have reached their deepest level of relaxation. If you wake a sleeper during level five, she will often report that she was dreaming. Although many of us don't remember much or anything about our dreams, sleep researchers have found that all of their subjects had several periods of REM sleep each night, so dreaming seems to be a normal and nightly occurrence.

Sleep research is a relatively young field and we still really don't know why humans need to sleep, but there is little doubt about how disruptive lack of good sleep can be. In particular it seems that we need levels three, four and REM sleep to function normally during the day. It has also been found that if you are somehow deprived of REM sleep, eventually your body will catch up by having lots of it. This *rebound effect* is usually marked by vivid dreams or nightmares—basically disturbed sleep. We have taken time to explain all this to you not because you need to be an instant expert on sleep theory, but because it affects what you do about disturbed sleep, as you will see.

How Much Sleep Do You Need?

Sleep needs vary a lot between different people and tend to decline with increasing age. Most newborn babies sleep seventeen to eighteen hours a day but by age ten this is down to nine to ten hours. Around two-thirds of adults sleep seven to eight hours a night, a fifth less than six hours, and a tenth more than nine hours. Although some insomnia sufferers complain they didn't sleep at all, researchers have found they usually do sleep for at least a few hours. Complete insomnia is a rare condition, particularly because researchers have found we can have *microsleeps*, brief periods of sleep during periods of wakefulness, so brief we don't notice them.

One bad night's sleep, even as little as two hours, doesn't really affect your performance the next day, although you may feel more irritable, hostile, fatigued or unhappy. Short sleep for a week makes some people pathologically sleepy, but even these cumulative effects disappear after one good night's sleep. So the real question is not how much time you spend asleep, but how you feel during the day. If your sleep disturbance is clearly connected to your crisis experience, you might expect it to fade as you work through your recovery. This is possible but there is one risk: Insomnia can become a habit.

> *One bad night's sleep, even as little as two hours, doesn't really affect your performance the next day.*

For some, insomnia was triggered by an easily identifiable cause: a painful illness, jetlag, a peak of stress, whatever. But after the original trigger has long faded from the person's life, she still has disturbed sleep because it has become a conditioned part of her life. She has learned that bed is a place where she vainly tries to sleep, and approaching sleep causes anxiety about "another sleepless night." She may also have tried some of the popular remedies for sleeping problems that actually make them worse, or developed some bad sleep habits that now keep her problem going. If you are having more than the occasional night of disturbed sleep and this is interfering with your daytime functioning, even if the disturbance is clearly a result of your crisis experience, we suggest you take some practical steps to sleep better to avoid the risk of developing a long-term sleeping problem. If you already had a sleeping problem, whether or not your crisis made it worse, you will benefit from sleep management.

What Disturbs Your Sleep?

Sleep researchers agree that insomnia is not an illness but a symptom of underlying problems, just as pain or a headache signifies something else is wrong. There are five factors that contribute to insomnia:

1. Biological factors

2. Psychological factors

3. Use of drugs, including alcohol

4. Disturbing environments and bad sleep habits

5. Conditioning

The specialists in treating sleep disorders agree on two more important points. First, they never see someone with a sleep disturbance due to only one of these possible factors. Significant sleep problems always reflect the interaction of several causes. Second, they agree that successfully solving a sleep problem requires carefully identifying the individual causes, so that you tackle all of those relevant to you. The point about these conclusions is that, even if your crisis reactions are clearly the main psychological factor contributing to your sleep problem, some of the other factors are involved as well. If you want to solve your sleeping problem now, you need to identify *all* of its possible causes and do something constructive about them. To help you self-diagnose and plan your personal sleep-management program, we will now describe those five possible factors and their implications.

Significant sleep problems always reflect the interaction of several causes.

Biological factors

Sleep and wakefulness are probably governed by two brain systems, an arousal system and a sleep system. For sleep to occur, the sleep system must override the arousal system. Psychologist Peter Hauri, who is director of the sleep disorders clinic at Dartmouth Medical School, believes that some insomniacs may have strong arousal systems or weak sleep systems. Compared with sound sleepers, insomniacs have higher levels of physiological arousal even when they are having a good night's sleep. They typically wake up more often, have faster heart rates and higher body temperatures. This basically means that your sleep will benefit if you are able to go to bed in a physically relaxed state.

Medical problems can also disturb sleep. Potential culprits are arthritis, ulcers, angina, migraines and other physical pain; asthma, sleep apnea (brief periods of not breathing) and other breathing disorders; irregular heartbeat; kidney disease; thyroid gland problems; pregnancy; and jerky spasms in your large muscles, especially the legs (called *nocturnal myoclonus*). Since these are medical problems, you should be getting medical treatment for them.

The normal, gradual decline in your sleep needs as you age can cause problems if you start to worry about not getting as much sleep as you used to. Unless it is associated with the daytime consequences of insomnia, however, sleeping less as you grow older is not a problem.

Psychological factors

Psychological problems probably contribute to insomnia by increasing your emotional arousal, which in turn increases your physiological arousal. Insomnia is a common symptom of high stress and, by interfering with daytime functioning, it can further add to stress. Some depressed people suffer from early morning waking, although some respond to their depression by sleeping more than usual. This is still a sleep disturbance because these people report being fatigued, despite their extra sleep.

Crises are themselves peaks of stress and may have consequences that keep your stress level high. Depression is probably the most common emotional reaction during the crisis recovery cycle, so it is not surprising that many crisis victims have sleep disturbances. You should already be following our suggestions from the previous chapter for managing your depression. How can you tell whether your sleep disturbance reflects only the stress of your crisis experience or a more

general problem with high stress? Try answering the
following questions:

- Do you often feel bad?

- Do you have trouble concentrating or remembering?

- Are you often sick?

- Are you having problems in your important relationships?

- Are you having trouble keeping up with important tasks?

- Do you often eat unhealthfully?

- Do you often drink too much alcohol?

- Do you smoke?

- Are you using any drug, prescribed or not, to lessen
  bad feelings?

The more times you answered "Yes," the more likely it is that
you are suffering from too much stress, although this simple
checklist won't tell you why. Many of these questions could reflect
your stress reactions to your crisis, so try to figure out if you would
have answered differently before your crisis experience. If most of
the questions you answered "Yes" to have started after your crisis,
you are probably having the normal stress reaction to being a crisis
victim. In that case, the program you have begun in this manual
should be enough.

On the other hand, if most of your "Yesses" would also have
been true before your crisis experience, your crisis may be adding
to a stress problem you already had. In that case, we suggest you
work through this book first. It's enough to keep you busy for
now. As a bonus to recovering successfully from your crisis, you
may also strengthen your coping skills generally and no longer
have a stress problem. If you still have a sleep problem after
completing this program, then we suggest you start some general
stress-management techniques, which you can find in a self-help
book focused exclusively on stress.

Drug use

Many drugs, including alcohol, can disturb your sleep. This includes legal and illegal drugs, prescribed, over-the-counter and social drugs. In one research study, drug or alcohol dependency was found to be a major cause of insomnia for one in eight sufferers. Sleep clinicians have found that many types of stimulants, sedatives and other mood-affecting drugs can disturb sleep. So can some of the drugs used for thyroid problems, contraception and heart disease. If you are taking any regular medication, you should ask your doctor if it might be contributing to your sleeping problem and, if so, whether you might try a different drug or even a nondrug treatment.

What may surprise you, however, is that sleeping drugs themselves contribute to sleep disturbance. That's right: The drugs that may be suggested to treat your sleeping problem can make it worse. This is obviously important and confusing: One "expert" is suggesting you take these drugs while some other "expert" (us) is suggesting you don't. So let us explain our doubts about sleeping drugs so you can make your own informed decision.

Sleeping drugs usually do put you to sleep and so they seem to work. The trouble is, they knock out the lower levels of sleep, the ones that are essential for your refreshment. They cause fragmented and disturbed sleep, shortened REM sleep periods and frequent early waking. Because of these unwanted side effects, you may spend time asleep without getting the benefit of normal sleep.

> *The drugs that may be suggested to treat your sleeping problem can make it worse.*

A further problem is that your body can become accustomed to the sleeping drug so that you have to keep increasing the dose to get any effect until even taking the maximum safe dose is no longer effective. Many people end up hooked on their sleeping drugs, with a drug dependency problem as well as an unsolved sleeping problem.

Because sleeping drugs reduce your REM sleep periods, if you stop taking the drug, you then have the rebound effect we described earlier, with vivid dreams and nightmares. Many people have misinterpreted this rebound sleep disturbance as meaning they needed to stay on their sleeping drug, because trying to go without it led to a terrible night's sleep. Then they were really hooked.

All of this criticism may seem harsh to you, so we repeat that we are not simply antidrug. These adverse findings are the result of medical, not psychological, research. Dr. German Nino-Murcia, the psychiatrist in charge of the sleep disorders clinic at Stanford University, said, only half-jokingly, "The best treatment for insomnia is to grab patients by the feet and shake until all the medications fall out of their pockets." We are critical of sleeping drugs because a lot of research and clinical experience show that they don't really help with sleeping problems.

Some medical practitioners have accepted this; instead of prescribing sleeping drugs, however, they prescribe an antianxiety drug "to help you sleep." We applaud their intentions, but the most common antianxiety drugs are a group called *benzodiazepines*. Unfortunately, researchers have found that you can get a rebound effect after using these drugs for as few as three nights. The risk is that the rebound sleeplessness prompts you to take more drugs the next night and you end up hooked on them again. Antianxiety drugs may help if you have had only a temporary problem with insomnia, but make sure you recognize what has caused your rebound, if you have one when you stop taking the drug. The experts in the field now agree that drugs are simply not the answer for serious or long-term insomnia.

We have referred to alcohol in this discussion because it is a popular form of self-help for insomnia, but it has the same undesirable effects as prescription sleeping drugs. You may spend time asleep, but it won't be normal, refreshing sleep. Two or three nights of excessive drinking are enough to give you rebound sleeplessness the next night. If you then reach for the bottle to get to sleep, you are well on your way to developing a drinking problem.

We are not going to discuss drinking problems in detail, but sadly they are sometimes the result of a mismanaged crisis. Try answering the following questions to determine if you have a problem with alcohol.

- Do you often have more than four alcoholic drinks a day, if you're a man, or two, if you're a woman?

- Would you find it difficult to go without alcohol for a day?

- When you do drink, do you tend to drink a lot?

- Has drinking interfered with your work?

- Has drinking interfered with your relationships?

- Has drinking damaged your health?

The more times you answered "Yes," the more likely it is that you have a drinking problem. Once again, try to figure out whether this has only happened since your crisis experience, in which case working through this program may be enough to restore your control over your drinking. Or did you really have a drinking problem before your crisis, even if the crisis made it worse? In that case, we recommend you tackle your drinking problem as well. If self-help for recovering from your crisis plus solving a drinking problem is too much to handle on your own, consider getting professional help or joining a recovery group, such as Alcoholics Anonymous (see the Resources section on page 215).

Weaning yourself off sleeping drugs

If you have been using a sleeping drug for a while, no matter how helpful it may have been, consider weaning yourself off it, unless you want to take it for the rest of your life. Your body is probably accustomed to the drug. If you just stop taking it, you will probably suffer from unpleasant withdrawal symptoms, including rebound sleeplessness. To avoid withdrawal symptoms, you should wean yourself off the drug slowly by gradually reducing the amount you take each day. Before you begin weaning yourself off a sleeping

To avoid withdrawal symptoms, you should wean yourself off the drug slowly by gradually reducing the amount you take each day.

drug, however, follow all the suggestions in this chapter that apply to you. That way, when you begin weaning, you will be managing your sleep as well as you can and minimize the chance of having disturbed sleep that might scare you back into taking the drug.

Some people can wean themselves off a long-term drug without much trouble, especially by doing it gradually. Hopefully your doctor will help you by suggesting a gradual reduction in dosage. Others have a harder time because they depend on the drug. They think things like, "I wonder if I'll sleep tonight if I only take half my usual dose?" Naturally this sort of worrying is likely to keep you awake and ruin your efforts to sleep without depending on drugs. If anxiety about reducing your dosage is likely to be a problem for you, then you need the help of a friend or family member.

Your helper's task is to provide you with a "drug cocktail" instead of your usual pills. It will contain your usual drug, but in amounts that decrease without your knowing when or how much, so that you can't talk yourself into withdrawal symptoms. Your helper can mix your drug with jam or honey or something similar, to disguise the actual dosage. Or you may find a helpful pharmacist willing to prepare some "cocktails" for you, in a syrup base. To begin, your helper provides a cocktail each night that contains your usual dose. After a few nights, your helper reduces the dose by, say, half a tablet, and gives you this cocktail for a few nights. The reductions should be made at irregular intervals, so that you don't know when your dose is really being reduced. Each dose level should be kept up for at least a few nights to give your body time to adapt. If you believe you are suffering from withdrawal effects, tell your helper and she can increase the dose back to the previous level, then reduce it again more gradually. After you have been taking a drug-free cocktail for a few nights, your helper can tell you and congratulate you for weaning yourself off an unnecessary drug.

Bad sleep habits or environments

As we mentioned earlier, dealing with biological insomnia involves going to bed in a physically relaxed state. Any habits that involve going to bed in an aroused state, or not needing sleep, can contribute to insomnia. It doesn't help if your stomach is rumbling from hunger, too much food or food that was too spicy or rich. Drinking caffeine, in coffee, tea or soda, will stimulate your arousal level. Carbohydrate-rich foods, like pasta or sweets, have been thought to have an arousing and energizing effect. In fact, researchers have found the opposite is true. A meal heavy in carbohydrates, especially when they are not balanced by other food groups such as proteins, usually has a calming and even fatiguing effect. Men tend to feel relaxed and women tend to feel sleepy. These effects are more noticeable in people over forty, but they also apply to children. The researchers pointed out that these were the effects of eating lots of carbohydrates in most people and were not due to hypoglycemia, which is actually a rare condition. Without sacrificing other important food groups in your overall diet, an increase in your carbohydrate consumption in the evening may help you sleep.

Reading exciting books or watching exciting television just before bed, or even in bed, won't help you nod off. Postponing important problem-solving discussions until lights out won't help, either, especially if they turn into arguments. Sexual interaction leaves most people feeling pleasant and relaxed, but if yours leaves you aroused, plan it for some other time. Being fit helps you sleep, but a vigorous exercise workout just before sleep probably won't.

Other habits to watch carefully involve how you time your sleep. Your body has its own natural rhythms of wakefulness and sleepiness, usually associated with daylight and dark. If you go to sleep and wake up at irregular times, you can throw those rhythms out of kilter. This is most obvious when you

> *Two of the worst sleep habits are to sleep in or to nap during the day in an attempt to catch up on sleep missed the night before.*

travel across time zones or change shifts at work, but some people do it to themselves by going to bed early one night and late the next. Two of the worst sleep habits are to sleep in or to nap during the day in an attempt to catch up on sleep missed the night before. You catch up, all right, but at the expense of your sleep needs the

next night. The traditional Sunday morning sleep-in is often
followed by Sunday night insomnia and Monday morning fatigue.

A noisy or uncomfortable sleep environment can contribute to
insomnia. Try to arrange the level of lighting and sound so that
they are comfortable for you. You may be surprised how much it
helps to put plugs in your ears if the noise in your environment is
out of your control. If your spouse snores, you may be doing him
a favor if you encourage him to seek help for it. Snoring is
sometimes associated with breathing irregularities during sleep that
are real health risks for the snorer. If you have been the victim of a
traumatic attack, especially at home, taking reasonable security
precautions may be important to help you relax. We give you some
more practical suggestions for developing good sleeping habits
starting on page 211.

Conditioning

If you don't do anything about your insomnia because you think it
will naturally fade as you recover from your crisis, you may be
conditioning yourself to sleep poorly
indefinitely. Having insomnia itself can
train you to be an insomniac, long after
the original cause of your disturbed
sleep has faded to a memory. The more
you associate being in bed with
struggling to sleep, the harder it
becomes for you to relax there.

The more you associate being in bed with struggling to sleep, the harder it becomes for you to relax there.

Eventually anything that signals that bedtime is approaching, such
as cleaning your teeth, can become a stimulus because it warns
you that the battle for sleep is about to begin again. In simple
terms, the more you learn to worry about not being able to sleep,
the more that worry will arouse you and stop you from sleeping.
Dr Peter Hauri found that 15 to 20 percent of the patients at the
Dartmouth sleep clinic were naturally light sleepers who, during
a period of stress, had learned bad sleep habits and became
conditioned to have insomnia even though the stress was gone.
If this applies to you, you will now need to reverse that
conditioning by following a sleep-management program.

Managing Your Sleep Better

In light of your reading above, pick from the following suggestions the ones that seem likely to help you sleep better. If you are not sure, you are better off trying a suggestion instead of leaving it out. Try out each suggestion for at least a week before you decide it isn't helping you. It takes time to change habits.

Learn to relax physically by going to a relaxation class or using a self-help tape. Researchers have found that all relaxation techniques—yoga, meditation, biofeedback, autogenic training, progressive relaxation—work equally well, so pick one that appeals to you. Use your relaxation skills to relax yourself in bed.

Try to have a regular bedtime with reasonable flexibility, but don't go to bed if you don't feel sleepy. Do something quiet and relaxing until you do.

If you're not falling asleep easily, don't worry about it. Try a coping statement instead, such as "Worrying about not going to sleep is a good way to keep myself awake. It's disappointing I'm not asleep yet, but I can cope with that. I won't deny my natural disappointment, but I won't arouse myself by worrying about not sleeping. Right now I'll use my relaxation skills to relax my body and I'll focus my mind on a pleasant fantasy."

And do both of those things.

A number of people have told us a relaxation tape gave them something to concentrate on, blocking out intrusive worries or memories. If you share your bed with someone, you can use a small headset to listen to the tape. Following the instructions for physical relaxation helps you to relax physically; occupying your mind with the instructions helps you to relax mentally.

If you are not asleep after half an hour, and you are becoming tense and frustrated, get up and go to another room. (If you are lying in bed relaxed and comfortable, stay there.) The same advice applies if you wake up during the night and don't easily go back to sleep. Do something quiet and relaxing until you feel sleepy and then go back to bed. Repeat this procedure as often as you need to. If that means you spend an hour sitting in the living room reading or listening to music, that's better than spending the

> *If that means you spend an hour sitting in the living room reading or listening to music, that's better than spending the same hour tossing and turning in bed.*

same hour tossing and turning in bed. A small snack helps some people go back to sleep and the research described above would favor a carbohydrate snack, such as bread, cake or rolls. Milk has been recommended in the past because it contains tryptophan, a natural sleep-inducing substance; however, some researchers now think that there isn't enough tryptophan in milk to help you sleep. Try it if you want to and decide for yourself.

Reduce alcohol, tobacco, chocolate, coffee, tea and caffeinated soft drinks in your diet, especially in the late afternoon and evening. If you think you are sensitive to caffeine, you may need to skip it altogether.

Keep fit with regular exercise. This will help you manage daytime stress better and reduce the fatigue that can actually make sleeping difficult or disturbed. Despite what you may believe about exercise, three half-hour workouts of moderate exercise a week are all you need for fitness (and better sleep).

Don't eat heavy meals just before bedtime. You may want the calming and sedating effect of a carbohydrate-rich meal, such as pasta for a main course or cake for dessert, but don't overdo the calories and make sure you give yourself time to digest it before bed. And we repeat our suggestion of moderate alcohol intake.

Reserve your bed for sleep, or sex if that leaves you feeling relaxed. Don't use bed as a place to worry, have important discussions or arguments, read or watch horror movies or otherwise arouse yourself. Plan those activities for other times and places.

Start a worries book, a small notebook in which you can write down ideas or problems as they occur to you, especially in the evening or during the night. Then you can use a coping statement: "I expect to feel aroused if I worry about that now, but I don't have to. I have written it on my list of things to deal with tomorrow and that's as much as I can do now. So now I'll use my relaxation skills and a pleasant fantasy to help myself sleep."

And do it.

It may help to jot down a brief plan of what you intend to do tomorrow, but don't be lured into doing your daytime problem-solving during your sleeping time.

Experiment with your bedroom atmosphere to find the sleeping environment best for you. Vary the light level. Try different temperatures. Does some quiet music help? Most clock-radios have a sleep button that switches the radio off after an hour or so. Should you change beds, in spite of the expense? We think a good waterbed is the greatest invention since sliced bread, but what do you find comfortable?

Get up at the same time each day. This is even more important than going to bed at the same time. Do *not* sleep in, even if you don't feel great for the rest of the day. You will only waste your sleep needs and upset your biological rhythms.

Do not nap during the day, for the same reasons. If you had a bad night's sleep, try to keep physically active rather than napping and you will help yourself sleep better the next night.

Manage your daytime stress by working on the rest of this book to aid your recovery from your crisis, especially chapter 8. If necessary, start some systematic stress management.

Get medical advice if you think any of the medical problems listed on page 203 may be disturbing your sleep. If you have been using drugs to help you sleep, discuss our advice with your doctor and consider weaning yourself off the drugs.

Sleeping problems can be difficult to treat in a clinic, so don't be upset if your self-help isn't enough. Tell yourself you don't have to put up with it and get professional help for your sleeping problems.

Resources

Alcohol and Drug Abuse

**Al-Anon Family Group
Headquarters, Inc.**
1600 Corporate Landing Pkwy.
Virginia Beach, VA 23454-5617
888-4AL-ANON
Website: www.al-anon.alateen.org/
*Information about Al-anon and
Alateen: groups for those coping
with someone else's drinking
problem*

Alcoholics Anonymous
800-640-7545
Website: www.alcoholics-
    anonymous.org/
*Call or see website for local AA
information in United States
and Canada*

**Bureau of Alcohol and
Drug Programs**
976 Lenzen Ave., 3rd Floor
San Jose, CA 95126
408-299-6141
Fax: 408-279-1843
Information and referral

Narcotics Anonymous
World Service Office in
    Los Angeles
P.O. Box 9999
Van Nuys, CA 91409
800-4-HELP-NA, 818-773-9999
Fax: 818-700-0700
Website: www.wsoinc.com/

Disasters

American Red Cross
Attn: Public Inquiry Office
1621 N. Kent St., 11th Floor
Arlington, VA 22209
703-248-4222
Website: www.redcross.org

The Canadian Red Cross Society
1430 Blair Place
Gloucester, ON K1J 9N2
613-740-1900
Fax: 613-740-1911
Email: cancross#redcross.ca

**Federal Emergency Management
Association (FEMA)**
500 C St. SW
Washington, DC 20472
Publications: 800-480-2520
Teleregistration (apply for
    disaster assistance if you
    live in a designated federal
    disaster area): 800-462-9029
Website: www.fema.gov

Grief

**Bereaved Parents of the USA
(BPUSA) National Headquarters**
P.O. Box 95
Park Forest, IL 60466
708-748-7672
Fax: 708-748-9184

**Bereavement Support
Services—Canada**
905-628-6008

Grief Recovery Hotline
800-445-4808

Teen Age Grief, Inc. (TAG)
P.O. Box 22034
Newhall, CA 91322
805-253-1932
Support for bereaved teenagers;
offers training for grief support
groups for teens

Illness

Alzheimer's Association, Inc.
919 N. Michigan Ave., Ste. 1000
Chicago, IL 60611
800-272-3900 (Illinois)
800-621-0379 (National)

American Cancer Society, Inc.
90 Park Ave.
New York, NY 10016
212-736-3030
Website: www.cancer.org

Canadian Mental Health
Associates
2160 Yonge St., 3rd Floor
Toronto, ON M4S 2Z3
416-484-7750

Canadian Cancer Society and
National Cancer Institute of Canada
10 Alcorn Ave., Ste. 200
Toronto, ON M4V 3B1
416-961-7223
Fax: 416-961-4189
Website: www.cancer.ca

Children's Hospice International
901 N. Washington St.
Alexandria, VA 22314
800-24CHILD

Hyacinth Foundation Support
800-433-0254
For AIDS patients and family
members

Leukemia Society of America
733 3rd Ave.
New York, NY 10017
212-573-8484

National Center for Post-
Traumatic Stress Disorder
VAM & ROC 116D
Rural Route 5
White River Junction, VT 05009
802-296-5132

National Organization for Rare
Disorders, Inc. (NORD)
P.O. Box 8923
New Fairfield, CT 06812-8923
800-999-6673, 203-746-6518
Fax: 203-746-6481

National SIDS Alliance
1314 Bedford Ave., Ste. 210
Baltimore, MD 21208
800-221-SIDS
Fax: 410-964-8009

Ronald McDonald House
212-876-1590

Menopause

American Menopause Foundation
350 Fifth Ave., Ste. 2822
New York, NY 10118
212-714-2398

Canadian Women's Health Network
419 Graham Ave., Ste. 203
Winnipeg, MT R3C 0M3
204-942-5500
Fax: 204-989-2355
Email: cwhn@cwhn.ca
Clearinghouse: 888-818-9172

The North American
Menopause Society
C/o Dept. of Ob/Gyn
University Hospitals of Cleveland
11100 Euclid Ave.
Cleveland, OH 44106
216-844-1000

Rape, Abuse and Incest Survivors

Center for the Prevention of Sexual and Domestic Violence
1914 N. 34th St., Ste. 105
Seattle, WA 98103
206-631-1903

The Healing Woman Foundation
P.O. Box 28040-W
San Jose, CA 95159
408-246-1788
Fax: 408-247-4309
Email: HealingW@
    healingwoman.org
Website: www.healingwoman.org
For women survivors of childhood sexual abuse

National Coalition Against Domestic Violence
P.O. Box 18749
Denver, CO 80218
303-839-1852
Hotline: 800-799-7233
Fax: 303-831-9251
Website: www.ncadv.org/

National Coalition Against Sexual Assualt
125 N. Enola Dr.
Enola, PA 17025
717-728-9764
Fax: 717-732-1575
Email: ncasa@redrose.net

National Women's Law Center
11 Dupont Circle, Ste. 800
Washington, DC 20036
202-588-5180
Website: www.afj.org/mem/
    nwlc.html
Advocates for women's rights in many areas

Rape, Abuse & Incest National Network
252 10th St. NE
Washington, DC 20002
202-544-1034
Hotline: 800-656-HOPE
Fax: 202-544-1401

Women's Bureau
800-827-5335
For victims of sexual assault

Women in Crisis Support Group
800-424-5600
For survivors of sexual abuse

Suicide Prevention

American Foundation for Suicide Prevention
120 Wall St., 22nd Floor
New York, NY 10005
888-333-AFSP, 212-363-3500
Fax: 212-363-6237

Suicide Awareness/Voices of Education (SA/VE)
P.O. Box 24507
Minneapolis, MN 55424-0507
612-946-7998
Email: save@winternet.com
Website: www.save.org/

Torture Survivors

Advocates for Survivors of Torture
Union Memorial Hospital
201 E. University Pkwy.
Baltimore, MD 21218
410-554-2504
Fax: 410-243-5642
    (attn. Karen Hanscom, Ph.D.)
Email: klh@igc.apc.org

Canadian Centre for Victims of Torture (CCVT)
194 Jarvis St., 2nd Floor
Toronto, ON M5B 2B7
416-480-0489
Fax: 416-480-1984
Email: CCVT@io.org

Center for Victims of Torture
John Salzberg, Washington
    Representative
605 G St. SW
Washington, DC 20024
202-484-0099
Fax: 202-424-0134

Troubled Children and Their Parents

"Because I Love You"©
The Parent Support Group
P.O. Box 473
Santa Monica, CA 90406-0473
888-443-4481, 310-659-5289,
 818-882-4881
Fax: 323-585-4762
Email: bily1982@aol.com
Website: www.becauseilove
 you.org/
*For parents of troubled children
of any age*

Child Welfare League of Canada
75 Albert St., Ste. 209
Ottawa, ON K1P 5E7
613-235-4412
Fax: 613-235-7616
Email: cwlc@newforce.ca
Website: www.cwlc.ca

KidsPeace®
The National Center for
 Kids Overcoming Crisis
800-8KID-123
Website: www.kidspeace.org/

Further Reading

Ainscough, Carolyn, and Kay Toon. *Surviving Childhood Sexual Abuse: Practical Self-Help for Adults Who Were Sexually Abused as Children.* Tucson, Ariz.: Fisher Books, 2000.

Benson, Herbert, M.D., and Miriam Z. Klipper. *The Relaxation Response.* New York: Avon, 1990.

Berry, Dawn Bradley. *The Domestic Violence Sourcebook : Everything You Need to Know.* Los Angeles: Lowell House, 1998

Buchwald, Emilie, Martha Roth and Pamela Fletcher, eds. *Transforming a Rape Culture.* Minneapolis, Minn.: Milkweed Editions, 1993.

Carnegie, Dale. *How to Stop Worrying and Start Living.* New York: Pocket Books, 1985.

Cerza Kolf, June. *Comfort & Care in a Final Illness: Support for the Patient & Caregiver.* Tucson, Ariz.: Fisher Books, 1999.

————. *How Can I Help? How to Support Someone Who Is Grieving.* Tucson, Ariz.: Fisher Books, 1999.

Davis, Martha, Elizabeth Robbins Eshelman and Matthew McKay. *Relaxation & Stress Reduction Workbook.* Oakland, Calif.: New Harbinger Publications, 1998.

De Becker, Gavin. *The Gift of Fear: Survival Signals That Protect Us from Violence.* New York: Dell Publishing Co., 1998.

Deits, Bob. *Life after Loss.* Tucson, Ariz.: Fisher Books, 1999.

Everstine, Diana, and Louis Everstine. *People in Crisis: Strategic Therapeutic Interventions.* New York: Brunner/Mazel, 1983.

Ferguson, Robert, and Jeanine Ferguson. *Guide to Rape Awareness and Prevention: Educating Yourself, Your Family and Those in Need.* Hartford, Conn.: Turtle Press, 1994

Ginsberg, Genevieve Davis, M.S. *Widow to Widow: Thoughtful, Practical Ideas for Rebuilding Your Life.* Tucson, Ariz.: Fisher Books, 1997.

Goldberger, L., and S. Breznitz, eds. *Handbook of Stress: Theoretical & Clinical Aspects.* New York: Free Press, 1993.

Graber, Ken. *Ghosts in the Bedroom: A Guide for Partners of Incest Survivors.* Deerfield Beach, Fla.: Health Communications, 1991.

Iacopi, Robert L. *Earthquake Country! How, Why and Where Earthquakes Strike in California.* Tucson, Ariz.: Fisher Books, 1996.

Israeloff, Roberta. *What to Do About Your Child's Moods and Emotions: Real Solutions from Expert Parents and Kids.* New York: Reader's Digest, 1998.

Jacobson, Neil S., Ph.D., and John Mordechai Gottman. *When Men Batter Women: New Insights into Ending Abusive Relationships.* New York: Simon & Schuster, 1998.

Johnston, Janet R. *In the Name of the Child: A Developmental Approach to Understanding and Helping Children of Conflicted and Violent Divorce.* New York: Free Press, 1997.

Kabat-Zinn, Jon, and Joan Borysenko. *Full Catastrophe Living: Using the Wisdom of Your Body and Mind to Face Stress, Pain, and Illness.* New York: Delacorte Press,1990.

Lothrop, Hannah. *Help, Comfort & Hope after Losing Your Baby in Pregnancy or the First Year.* Tucson, Ariz.: Fisher Books, 1997.

Marshall, Fiona. *Losing a Parent: Practical Help for You and Other Family Members.* Tucson, Ariz.: Fisher Books, 2000.

O'Connor, Richard. *Undoing Depression: What Therapy Doesn't Teach You and Medication Can't Give You.* Boston: Little, Brown, 1997

Parkinson, Frank. *Post-Trauma Stress: Restore Your Emotional Health.* Tucson, Ariz.: Fisher Books, 2000.

Pearsall, Paul, Ph.D. *A Healing Intimacy: The Power of Loving Connections.* New York: Crown Trade Paperbacks, 1995.

Potter-Efron, Ron, and Patricia S. Potter-Efron. *Letting Go of Anger: The 10 Most Common Anger Styles and What to Do About Them.* Oakland, Calif.: New Harbinger Publications, 1995.

Raphael, Beverley. *The Anatomy of Bereavement: A Handbook for the Caring Professions.* Northvale, N.J.: Jason Aronson, 1994.

Schnarch, David. *Passionate Marriage: Love, Sex, and Intimacy in Emotionally Committed Relationships.* New York: Henry Holt, 1998.

Schnebly, Lee, M.Ed. *I Do? Being Happy, Being Married.* Tucson, Ariz.: Fisher Books, 1994.

Warshaw, Robin. *I Never Called It Rape: The Ms. Report on Recognizing, Fighting, and Surviving Date and Aquaintance Rape.* New York: Harperperennial Library, 1994.

Index

A

accidents, 31–32

adolescents. *See* teenagers

affairs. *See* extra-marital affairs

aggression, 189–190

alcohol. *See also* drugs

   contributing to sleep problems, 205–207

   contributing to violent behavior, 60–61

   using to recover from a crisis, 127–129

anger, 129–130, 186–194

   arguments caused by, 192–194

   causes of, 188–190

   defined, 187

   emotional response following crisis, 8

   emotional response following suicide, 55

   managing, 190–192

   when becomes problem, 187–188

antianxiety drugs, using for sleep problems, 206

arguments, 58. *See also* family conflicts

   anger and, 192–194

B

battered children, 66–69

battered women, 59, 64–66

   common pattern of, 65

behavior, asking for changes by, 170–172

   listening, 172–174

   making effective requests, 171–172

   validating, 174–176

bladder control, loss of, 4

body talk, 161–162, 176–177

bowel control, loss of, 4

C

calming response, 152–154

   using when angry, 190–191

captivity, being held in, 29–30

child abuse. *See also* incest

   battered children, 66–69

   sexual abuse and incest, 69–73

   signs child has been victim of, 71–73

child, death of

   grief process and, 49–51

chronic illness

   coping with, 35–38

   managing, 38–39

   nurturing important relationships, 40–41

   seeking alternative therapies, 38–39

chronic pain

   common traps sufferers fall into, 43

   coping statements to help, 44

   managing, 41–44

   psychological components of, 41–42

communication, maintaining good, 177–178

conflict, defined, 57–58

confronting your hurt, 11

coping statements, 134–139, 154, 156, 158

   defined, 135

   elements of, 135–139

   using to help fall asleep, 211

   using to manage guilt, 195–196

writing down, 135
counseling, how soon should begin
    following crisis, ix
crisis
    basic plan for coping with, 119
    coping statement, 134–139
    coping with, 119–131
        accept emotional support, 123–126
        accept normal reactions, 119–120
        getting organized, 122–123
        group sharing, 120–122
        organizations helping with, 126–127
        share feelings, 120
        using resources available, 123–126
    defined, 1
    drugs and alcohol, warnings
        regarding use of, 127–129
    emotional reactions to, 1–3
    physical reactions to, 4, 130
    variability of reactions, 2–3
crisis response, 3–6
    defined, 3
    disbelief, 4–5
    non-emotional survival state, 5–6
    realization, 5
    recovery, 6
    release, 6
Crisis Response and Recovery Cycle
    (CRRC), 3–12. *See also* recovery cycle
    personal disasters and, 13
CRRC. *See* Crisis Response and
    Recovery Cycle

D

death, 33–41. *See also* grief
    of child, coping with, 49–51
    fear of, 9, 34
    impending, coping with, 34–38
    of unborn child, grief process and,
        51–54
denial, using coping statement to
    overcome, 136, 138

depression, 129–130, 179–186
    causes of, 181–182
    as emotional reaction to chronic
        illness, 36–37
    as emotional response following
        crisis, 7
    managing, 182–185
    menopause and, 86–89
    physical treatment for, 180–181
    questions to ask, 179–180
    suicide and, 185–186
disaster syndrome, 105
disasters, large-scale
    community preparation programs,
        112
    defined, 99
    emotional reactions during, 104–106
    emotional reactions following,
        106–108
    emotions experienced at
        approaching, 101, 102–103
    escape as first response, 105
    heroic actions, taking 105
    man-made disasters, emotional
        reactions to, 109–110
    natural disasters, emotional reactions
        to, 109–110
    post-crisis counseling for, 99
    premonitions of, 103
    preparation for, 100–101
    recovering from, 111–115
    rescuers reactions to, 113–114
    stages of, 100–101
    stress debriefings for rescuers,
        113–115
disbelief, as emotional response to
    crisis, 4–5
distraction activity, using to respond to
    crisis, 138–139
divorce, 78

drugs. *See also* alcohol
  as contributing factor in violence, 60
  disturbing sleep, 205–207
  to treat depression, 180
  using to recover from a crisis,
    127–129
dwelling on bad feelings
  using coping statements to
    overcome, 137–139

E

effective requests, using to change
  behavior, 171–172
emotional support, using for recovery,
  123–126
emotions, managing constructively, 161
Everstine, Dr. Diane, 17–18
Everstine, Dr. Louis, 17–18
extra-marital affairs, 74–78
  choices to make, 77

F

family
  helping recover from a crisis, 11–12,
    123–126
  support for in grief process, 49
  violence in home, 59–63
family conflicts, 57–63
  alcohol and drugs contributing to,
    60–61
  cycle of, 61, 63
  fights, 58–63
  resources, 223
  teenagers and, 73–74
fear, as initial reaction following
  violent crime, 14
feelings, sharing
  body talk, 176–177
  expressing through leveling, 162–169
  listening, 172–174
  maintaining effective communication,
    177–178

  validating, 174–176
females, psychological effects of
  violent crime on, 18–19
friends. *See also* family
  helping recover from a crisis, 11–12,
    123–126
  support from during grief process, 49

G

goals
  characteristics for successful, 83–85
  setting for employment possibilities,
    86–97
  setting life goals, 82–86
grief, 44–56. *See also* death
  death of child, 49–51
  death of unborn child, 51–54
  following suicide, 54–56
  managing, 48–49
  religious beliefs and, 33–34
  shadow, 51
  stages of, 45–47
  unresolved, complications from,
    47–48
group sharing, 120–122
  stress debriefings and, 121
guilt, 129–130, 194–197
  as emotional reaction to suicide, 55
  managing, 195–197

H-I

Hearst, Patty, 30
hostage, being held, 29–30
illness, life-threatening
  emotional reactions to, 35–38
  managing, 38–39
  nurturing important relationships,
    40–41
  seeking alternative therapies, 38–39
incest, 69–73
  long-term effects of, 71
  signs child has been victim of, 71–73

statistics on, 69
insomnia, 199, 201–211. *See also* sleep
  bad sleep habits, 209–210
  biological factors, 202–203
  conditioning yourself to sleep
    poorly, 210–213
  drugs and, 205–210
  foods contributing to, 209
  psychological factors, 203
  questions to ask, 204
  stress and, 203–204
irrational beliefs, 147–149, 155
  guilt and, 196

J-K

job, losing your, 92–97
  being fired, 93–94
  being laid off, 93–94
  goal-setting, 96–97
  retirement, 93–97
"John Wayne" syndrome, 124

L

leveling with others, 162–168
  about feelings, 162
  leveling statements, 164–170
  when not to, 168–169
life crisis, defined, vii
life goals, setting, 82–86
  jellyfish approach, 82
listening, using as communication tool,
  172–174

M

man-made disasters, 109–110.
  See also disasters, large-scale
marriage
  divorce and, 78
  extra-marital affairs, 74–78
  forced moves, effect on, 89
  menopause and, 87
  separation and, 78
menopause, 86–89

depression during, 86–89
  male, 88
mental relaxation, 133–134, 139–143
  practical exercises to help with,
    140–142
  report form, examples, 154–159
midlife crisis, 80–82
  setting life goals, 82–86
mood swings, 129–130
  emotional response following a
    crisis, 7–8
moving to new home, 89–92
  forced moves, 89–92

N-O

natural disasters, 109–110.
  See also disasters, large-scale
non-emotional survival state, 5–6
nonverbal communication, 161–162.
  See also body talk
nonvictims of violent crime, why
  unhelpful to victims, 19–21
organizing, as way to cope with a
  crisis, 122–123

P

pain, managing chronic, 41–44
personal disasters, coping with, 13–32
philosophical reflection, 8–11, 130–131
  vulnerability, realizing, 8–10, 130–131
post-traumatic stress disorders (PTSD),
  17, 110–111
pregnancy, terminated, grief process
  and, 51–54
prolonged terror, 29–30

R

rape victims, 21–25
  law and, 26–29
  nonvictims support for, 25–26
  partners support for, 26, 28
  psychological effects on, 18–19,
    24–25

reporting, 27–28

rational ideas, 149–152, 155, 257

practical exercises, 151

rational thinking, 142–143

realization, as emotional response to crisis, 5

recovery

as emotional response to crisis, 6

ingredients for successful, 12

recovery cycle, 7–12

anger, 8, 186

depression, 7

laying to rest, 11

mood swings, 7–8

philosophical reflection, 8–11

sharing feelings during, 163

shock, 7

relationships, nurturing, when faced with impending death, 40–41

relatives. *See* family

relaxation techniques, 42

mental relaxation, 133–134, 139–143, 154–159

muscular relaxation, 133–134

self-talk and, 143–144

as sleep aid, 211–212

release, as emotional response to crisis, 6

religious beliefs, role in grief process, 33–34

retirement, 93–97

rewarding activities, 40, 183–184

robbery, psychological effects on victims, 18–19

S

self-blaming, as reaction to violent crime, 15–16

self-talk , as coping mechanism, 37–38, 144–146

for chronic pain, 42–43

mental relaxation report forms, 154–159

practical exercises, 144

unrealistic, 62

sexual abuse, 69–73. *See also* incest

sexual molestation, victims of, 29

psychological effects on, 18–19

shame, 197. *See also* guilt

shock

as emotional response to a crisis, 4, 7

as emotional response to a large-scale disaster, 104

physiological components of, 4

sleep. *See also* insomnia

defined, 200

how much needed, 200–201

problems, 129–130, 210–213

foods contributing to, 209

managing, 210–213

medical problems causing, 203

rebound sleeplessness, 200, 206, 207

weaning off sleeping drugs, 207–208

Stockholm syndrome, 5–6, 29–30

stress

as cause of insomnia, 203–204

management techniques, 39

potential problems caused by, viii

stress debriefings, following large-scale disasters

for groups, 121

for rescuers, 113–115

suicide

depression and, 185–186

emotional reactions and, 55

female victims of crime and, 18–19

grief process and, 51–54

T

teenagers
  family conflicts and, 73
  life crises and, 74
  sexual abuse and, 73
thinking. *See also* rational thinking
  common mistakes in, 145
  irrational beliefs in, 147–149
torture, 31
tranquilizers, caution regarding use of,
  48
traumatic crisis. *See* personal disasters

U-V

unborn child, death of
  grief process and, 51–54
validating, 174–176
violent crimes, victims of
  effect on female victims, 18–19
  factors that influence severity of
    reaction, 17–18
  initial impact, 14–15
  long-term reactions to, 17
  nonvictims of, offering support to
    victims, 19–21
  professional support for victims,
    20–21
  reactions to, 13–18
  recoil stage, 14–16
  resolution stage, 17
vulnerable, feeling, emotional response
  following a crisis, 8–10, 130–131